DRAMA CLASSICS

THE RIVALS

by
Richard Brinsley Sheridan

introduced by
Colin Counsell

NICK HERN BOOKS
London

A Drama Classic

This edition of *The Rivals* first published in Great Britain
as a paperback original in 1994 by Nick Hern Books Limited,
14 Larden Road, London W3 7ST

Copyright in the introduction © 1994 Nick Hern Books Ltd

Typeset by Country Setting, Woodchurch, Kent TN26 3TB
Printed in Great Britain by BPC Wheatons Ltd, Exeter

A CIP catalogue record for this book is available from the
British Library

ISBN 1 85459 099 5

DRAMA CLASSICS

The Drama Classics series aims to offer the world's greatest plays in affordable paperback editions for students, actors and theatregoers. The hallmarks of the series are accessible introductions, uncluttered and uncut texts and an overall theatrical perspective.

Given that readers may be encountering a particular play for the first time, the introduction seeks to fill in the theatrical/historical background and to outline the chief themes rather than concentrate on interpretational and textual analysis. Similarly the play-texts themselves are free of footnotes and other interpolations: instead there is an end-glossary of 'difficult' words and phrases.

The texts of the English-language plays in the series have been prepared taking full account of all existing scholarship. The foreign language plays have been newly translated into a modern English that is both actable and accurate: many of the translators regularly have their work staged professionally.

Under the editorship of Kenneth McLeish, the Drama Classics series is building into a first-class library of dramatic literature representing the best of world theatre.

Series editor: Kenneth McLeish

Associate editors:
Professor Trevor R. Griffiths, *School of Literary and Media Studies, University of North London*
Simon Trussler, *Reader in Drama, Goldsmiths' College, University of London*

DRAMA CLASSICS *the first hundred*

The Alchemist
All for Love
Amphitryon
Andromache
Antigone
Arden of Faversham
Bacchae
The Bad-tempered
    Man
The Beaux' Stratagem
The Beggar's Opera
Birds
Blood Wedding
Brand
The Broken Jug
The Changeling
The Cherry Orchard
Children of the Sun
El Cid
The Country Wife
Cyrano de Bergerac
The Dance of Death
Doctor Faustus
A Doll's House
The Duchess of Malfi
Edward II
Electra (Euripides)
Electra (Sophocles)
An Enemy of the
    People
Enrico IV
The Eunuch
Every Man in his
    Humour
Everyman
The Father
Faust
A Flea in her Ear
Frogs
Fuenteovejuna

The Game of Love and
    Chance
Ghosts
The Government
    Inspector
Hedda Gabler
The Hypochondriac
The Importance of
    Being Earnest
An Italian Straw Hat
The Jew of Malta
King Oedipus
Life is a Dream
The Lower Depths
The Lucky Chance
Lulu
Lysistrata
The Magistrate
The Malcontent
The Man of Mode
The Marriage of
    Figaro
Mary Stuart
The Master Builder
Medea
Menaechmi
The Misanthrope
The Miser
Miss Julie
Molière
A Month in the
    Country
A New Way to Pay
    Old Debts
Oedipus at Kolonos
The Oresteia
Phaedra
Philoctetes
The Playboy of the
    Western World

The Revenger's
    Tragedy
The Rivals
The Robbers
La Ronde
The Rover
The School for Scandal
The Seagull
The Servant of Two
    Masters
Spring's Awakening
She Stoops to Conquer
The Shoemaker's
    Holiday
Six Characters in Search
    of an Author
Strife
Tartuffe
Thérèse Raquin
Three Sisters
'Tis Pity she's a Whore
Too Clever by Half
Ubu
Uncle Vanya
Vassa Zheleznova
Volpone
The Voysey
    Inheritance
The Way of the World
The White Devil
The Wild Duck
Women Beware
    Women
Women of Troy
Woyzeck
Yerma

*The publishers welcome
suggestions for further titles*

Introduction

Richard Brinsley Sheridan (1751-1816)

Sheridan was born in Dublin in 1751. His father, Thomas, was an actor, theatre manager and writer of popular farce, and his mother, Frances, was a novelist and playwright. In 1754 the family emigrated to England, and Sheridan became a pupil at Harrow School eight years later. In 1770 he moved with his father to Bath, the spa town that was to provide the setting for *The Rivals*.

Bath was established between 1760 and 1810 specifically as a resort for the well to do. Although people visited the town ostensibly to take its health-giving waters, it also provided an opportunity for mixing with other members of fashionable society, and for viewing prospective marriage partners. It was here that the young Sheridan met Elizabeth Linley, the professional singer who later became his wife. At the time she was engaged to be married to a wealthy and much older man, a contract that dissolved in scandal, providing Bath and London society with a topic for gossip for many months to come; the dramatist Samuel Foote even wrote a play based upon the event, *The Maid of Bath*. The scandal was not over, for Linley then became the subject of unwanted attention from another suitor, such that she determined to enter a French convent and actually travelled to France before being persuaded to return. Sheridan travelled with her and on their return he took her part, fighting two duels with the suitor. On 13 April 1773 Sheridan and Linley married and, lacking means to support a wife, Sheridan turned his eye to the stage.

On 17 January 1775 Sheridan's first play, *The Rivals,* was staged at the Covent Garden theatre in London. Although by no means autobiographical, *The Rivals* depicts many of the kinds of events that had coloured Sheridan's life: duels, frantic flights abroad, troubled love affairs. After its first performance the play was scorned by critics;

it was too long, and its characters were depicted in too cynical a fashion for the sensibilities of eighteenth century London. Encouraged by Covent Garden's proprietor, Thomas Harris, Sheridan rewrote the play in ten days, shortening it and redrawing the offending figures. The next version was a success.

Over the next four years Sheridan wrote five more plays, *St Patrick's Day* (1775), *The Duenna* (1775), *The Camp* (1775) *School for Scandal* (1777), and *The Critic* (1779), all of which were acclaimed. In 1776 he was able to buy a share in the Drury Lane theatre from its owner, the famous actor David Garrick, and Sheridan became Manager. In 1780 he was elected as Member of Parliament for Stafford, and from then on combined his theatrical career with a political one. His last play, the tragedy *Pizzaro*, was written in 1799 and proved one of his most successful.

In Sheridan's later years, however, his fortunes fell. The Drury Lane theatre burned down in 1809 and Sheridan was ousted from his position as manager in the theatre built to take its place. In 1812 he lost his parliamentary seat, and subsequently faced arrest for debt. On 17 July 1816 Sheridan died, by now a neglected figure. After his death, however, he was eulogised by the likes of Byron and Hazlitt and, as a result, his achievement was finally recognised.

Drama and Society

The eighteenth century is often referred to as 'The Age of Reason' or the 'Enlightenment', for it was during this time that Science and Rationalism in Europe developed into something resembling their modern forms. Perhaps Sir Isaac Newton best expressed many of the key concerns of the time by providing an image of the physical universe as a vast and beautiful machine, infinitely complex, perfectly integrated, and functioning according to natural laws laid down by God. This was an age in which the classical civilisations of Greece and, particularly, Rome were taken to represent an ideal of order, grandeur and civilised achievement, a model for contemporary endeavour. In Britain, the estates of the wealthy were landscaped to an arcadian perfection, poetry was sculpted into the measured and graceful form of the 'heroic couplet', while painting developed according to neoclassical principles formalised by Joshua Reynolds and the Royal Academy.

Such ideals of order and balance take on a different significance, perhaps, when we consider that in social and political terms this was a turbulent period. European wars were fought between Britain, France and Spain, and colonial conflicts erupted in America, Africa and Asia, while from 1789 the English ruling classes lived with the fear that the French Revolution might be exported across the Channel. At home, the enclosure of formerly public lands into private hands enlarged the estates of the rich but forced many peasants and smallholders into penury. The early stages of industrial development caused massive social upheaval as old communities and patterns of life were destroyed. Stripped of their livelihood, a stream of people moved from the countryside to seek new employment in cities and towns ill-equipped to receive them, resulting in widespread hardship.

The latter part of the century, when Sheridan lived and worked, was an age of both material and moral 'improvement' which saw the building of a network of roads and canals that facilitated trade and mobility, as well as growing literacy amongst the population, and developments in medicine, sanitation and agriculture. In parallel with such material progress, contemporary commentators record a growing belief that society and human nature itself was improving. Compassion and a sense of civic duty were deemed admirable qualities: in the words of a London magistrate, Sir John Hawkins, 'We live in an age when humanity is in fashion.'

It is in this context that drama such as Sheridan's developed. While Renaissance and Restoration plays continued to be mainstays of the late eighteenth-century stage, dubious material had to be rewritten in line with the audience's new propriety; characters were made more laudable, the satire was made less biting, and explicit sexual refer- ences were removed. The eighteenth century also saw the develop- ment of 'Sentimental Comedy', a genre with an altogether gentler and more tolerant view of humankind. In sentimental dramas events were always guided to a happy conclusion by a benign (and often improbable) providence, wicked characters would be reformed, and good hearts featured more frequently than savage wits.

Sentimentalism did not go unchallenged. In 1773 the playwright Oliver Goldsmith anonymously published his 'Essay on the Theatre', arguing in favour of a 'laughing comedy' which, instead of 'flattering every man in his favourite foible', would take the traditional comic path of 'ridiculously exhibiting the Follies of the Lower part of Mankind'. It is the plays of precisely those dramatists who took this path, Goldsmith and Sheridan, that still find a place on the modern stage – and among the most frequently performed of their works is *The Rivals*.

The Rivals: **What Happens in the Play**

The rivals of the title are suitors for the hand of Lydia Languish, a young woman of good family who holds to an impossible ideal of love. Opposed to any 'sensible' match with a man of comparable fortune, she will agree to marry only a pauper because, as this will mean forfeiting her own dowry, she will thereby ensure a life of romantic poverty. As a consequence the play's hero, Jack Absolute, is forced to adopt the guise of a poverty-stricken soldier, Ensign Beverley, in order to woo her. Meanwhile Jack's father, Sir Anthony Absolute, is also making plans for his son's future and approaches Lydia's aunt and guardian, Mrs Malaprop, to arrange a match between Jack and her ward. Jack has to appear both as Beverley and himself, and in both these identities is challenged to duel with his rival suitors, the country squire Bob Acres, and Sir Julius O'Trigger, a penniless Irish fortune-hunter. As the action unfolds Jack and Lydia's own romance is counterpointed thematically by that of their respective friends, Faulkland and Julia, whose own relationship undergoes similar emotional trials before the play's final, happy resolution.

Comedy of Manners and Comedy of Character

The Rivals is in part a Comedy of Manners, a lampoon upon all that is superficial and ephemeral in society: fashion, posturing and the affecting of over-elaborate social etiquette. Like the Restoration comedies of the seventeenth century, Sheridan's play takes as its particular target those who have pretensions to 'wit' and sophistication but lack the qualities necessary to make good their claim. The humour therefore derives from the difference between the image characters have of themselves and the picture they actually present to the world, between the pose and the reality.

Bob Acres, a character reminiscent of numerous comic country squires of the English stage, is a case in point. Entering the social world of Bath, Acres aims to cut a dash with his fashionable new clothes and coiffured hair which, he assures Jack Absolute, 'has been in training for some time'. By such means the squire of Clod Hall believes he will win the hand of Lydia Languish. But his 'side curls are a little restive' and his clothes clownish, for Acres is the quintessential country buffoon, an innocent adrift in sophisticated Bath society. Falling under the influence of the warlike Sir Lucius O'Trigger, he is easily cajoled into challenging his rival, the fictional Beverley, to a duel. But although his valour is stirred by the prospect, 'Fighting Bob' proves less enthusiastic when confronted with the reality of a naked sword.

Acres's unrealisable pretensions are rivalled only by those of Sheridan's most enduring creation, Mrs Malaprop, whose name has itself become a part of the English language. With her over-elaborate diction and references to scientific knowledge, Mrs Malaprop seeks to present herself as a woman of wit and learning. But the pose is wrecked by her continual misuse of words; she describes the intransigent Lydia, for instance, as 'headstrong as an allegory on the banks of the Nile'. Such 'malapropisms' sometimes prove truer than she knows. Referring to her own speech as 'a nice derangement of epitaphs', Mrs Malaprop displays the central quality of all characters in the Comedy of Manners tradition: a pretension whose hollowness only they are unable to see.

The full impact of such characterisations becomes apparent only when we place them on the Georgian stage, for the stage itself was an overtly artificial place (for a detailed description of theatre conditions, see page xvi). Although its painted backdrops were often spectacular and contained great realistic detail, they were, nevertheless, flat. Moreover, acting took place on the projecting forestage in close proximity to the side boxes and the front rows of the pit, without the physical distance and the resulting detachment necessary for fully-fledged 'illusion'. As is apparent from *The Rivals*, the closeness of actors to audience allowed dramatists to employ numerous comic asides, revealing the character's thoughts or comments on the action directly to the audience. More than any other eighteenth-century playwright, Sheridan was a master of artifice, and his particular skill lay in juxtaposing social façades against theatrical ones. When Mrs Malaprop takes the stage, or Bob Acres in his 'fashionable' clothes, the falsity of their poses is made more emphatic by a scenic design which is equally extravagant and every bit as contrived.

Sheridan sometimes goes further, making humorous allusions to the conditions of the theatre in the play's own action. This is evident in Act III, Scene iii, where Jack Absolute calls upon Mrs Malaprop for the first time to court Lydia under his own name. When Mrs Malaprop exits to fetch her niece, Jack turns to peruse the pictures hanging on the wall. But the 'wall' is a backcloth with the framed paintings painted onto it, and the backcloth is itself 'framed' by the stage's proscenium arch. When Lydia enters, she sees Jack from behind and, in an aside, judges him inferior to her true love Beverley; the illusion of the stage, called to the audience's attention by Jack's inspection of the painted 'paintings', is paralleled by the illusion fostered in Lydia's loving gaze. As the scene develops, Jack explains to Lydia that he, Beverley, has duped Mrs Malaprop into believing he is Jack Absolute. Mrs Malaprop emerges to eavesdrop on the lovers, but, believing Lydia to be rejecting Jack, she misinterprets everything; hearing Jack voice his concern that Lydia's 'warmth' has 'abated', Mrs Malaprop responds with 'so she has been in a passion . . . An ill-tempered little devil'. The scene ends with Lydia declaring her love for Beverley and Mrs Malaprop castigating her for such cruel treatment of a patient suitor. The niece is playing a joke on her aunt, yet Lydia herself is subject to a ruse to which only Jack and the audience are privy. In a play whose plot is founded upon dissembling and disguise, illusions, deceptions and misinterpretations overlap, drawing characters, the theatre and the audience itself into a kaleidoscope of façades.

In addition to being a Comedy of Manners, *The Rivals* is more importantly a comedy of character, where the comic situations result from the personality quirks of the play-world's occupants. This species of comedy has a long lineage. A century and a half before, it was believed by doctors that personality was determined by the proportions in one's body of various fluids or 'humours' – blood, choler, black bile and phlegm; an excess of phlegm made for a 'phlegmatic' nature, too much black bile made one 'melancholic', and so on. In the early seventeenth century the dramatist Ben Jonson developed a dramatic form known as the 'Comedy of Humours' wherein laughter was derived from these kinds of extreme personality traits, a tradition further refined in the Restoration Comedy of the second half of that century.

Although the 'scientific' theory of humours had been discredited by Sheridan's time, the comic strategy derived from it continued to exert a major influence upon drama. Thus *The Rivals* features a number of exaggerated 'types' and eccentrics, some of which had appeared in the English theatre for more than a century. Jack Absolute's friend Faulkland is quite a novel figure – the hypersensitive lover, cast into torment by his own imaginings – but in the extremity of his personality he is clearly cast in the 'humours' mould. Other characters are more traditional. Sir Anthony Absolute, the bad tempered and tyrannical father, has numerous theatrical antecedents, and Sir Lucius O'Trigger is the archetypical Irish gentleman of the literature of the time, aggressive and amorous, determined either to win Lydia or to exact his revenge upon Jack. Indeed most of the play's characters exemplify one of English comedy's 'types', with Acres as the country bumpkin, Mrs Malaprop the amorous grand dame, and Lucy the crafty and unreliable servant.

Sheridan emphasises these characters' exaggerated qualities by pairing them with their opposites. Thus we are treated to several scenes in which Mrs Malaprop's verbal chaos is compared with the linguistic precision of Sir Anthony, while Julia's sensible approach to love is posed against Lydia's naive romanticism. The dashing yet prudent Jack Absolute is a perfect foil to both the cloddish Acres and the overwrought Faulkland. Such pairings are more effective in the theatre than on the printed page. On stage, dialogue is augmented by the appropriate tones of voice, movement, posture and costume to create coherent characters. The characters's defining qualities are thereby rendered more emphatic, and so stand out in greater relief when shown alongside characters of a different nature.

At the first performance, critics found the characters of Sir Anthony and Sir Lucius objectionable. In his original form Sir Anthony was more lecherous, dwelling at length on Lydia's sexual attractiveness, while the drawing of the stereotypical Irishman Sir Lucius was described in the *Morning Post* as an 'ungenerous attack upon a nation'. In the rewritten play both were made more sympathetic. Indeed, none of the characters are subject to the kind of harsh satirisation characteristic of comedy in the previous century. Even the stock characters are given good qualities as well as bad. Sir Lucius, the fiery baronet of Blunderbuss Hall, takes the failure of his own suit with good grace, telling Jack that 'as I have been disappointed myself, it will be very hard if I have not the satisfaction of seeing other people succeed better'. Equally, although Bob Acres is shown to be a coward and a blusterer, he behaves magnanimously at Jack's victory, arranging an entertainment in honour of the engaged couple. Although *The Rivals* has heroes there are ultimately no villains, and all are included in its final vision of harmony. In line with eighteenth century theatrical convention, the final scene would have ended with all the characters lining up at the front of the stage to face into the auditorium, presenting the audience with a visual representation of concord to complement the play's own happy resolution.

Love and Money

Like so many comedies of the seventeenth and eighteenth centuries, *The Rivals* is concerned with the differing attitudes of the characters, young and old, to love, marriage and money. Both Sir Anthony and Mrs Malaprop demand that the young lovers accept the marriage partners that have been arranged for them. Sir Anthony is 'absolute' indeed, a man who will not allow his will to be thwarted (as is apparent from the first scene when we learn that he has dragged his family and retainers to Bath without notice, 'off at an hour's warning'). He is equally dogmatic in his demand that Jack marry the girl chosen for him (not yet revealed as Lydia), regarding obedience as a matter of familial duty. When Jack demurs, Sir Anthony reveals his wilful nature, comically warning his son 'take care – you know I am compliance itself – when I am not thwarted; no one more easily led – when I have my own way.'

This provides an opportunity for the kind of ironic reversal at which Sheridan excels. On learning that his proposed bride is Lydia herself, Jack returns to his father, artfully pretending contrition and declaring that he will obey Sir Anthony's will however old or ugly the bride. When his father objects to such unmanly compliance, saying 'When I was your age . . . I would not have touched anything old or ugly to gain an empire', Jack is able to turn Sir Anthony's own views against him; 'Not to please your father, Sir?'. This reversal is very apparent in performance because the similarity of the two scenes calls for their comparison: both feature Sir Anthony and Jack only, are concerned with plans for Jack's marriage to Lydia, and show Sir Anthony working himself into a temper.

While Sir Anthony's tyrannical attitude towards his son is clearly a burlesque, it reflects a reality of Sheridan's world. For the middle and upper classes marriage was a financial as well as personal arrangement, and parents took a keen interest in the prospects of their children's potential mates. Sir Anthony's description of Jack's engagement as a 'business' that must be 'foreclosed' is apt, for an advantageous match could maintain or advance a family's standing, and such considerations often prevailed over the personal wishes of the prospective partners.

In taking a critical view of such practices, *The Rivals* follows a long tradition of English comedy. Sir Anthony's comment to Jack that 'if you have the estate, you must take it with the live stock on it' is a comic exaggeration, effectively revealing his conception of women as items of barter within the marriage negotiation while at the same time ridiculing that view. Although Mrs Malaprop is a woman herself, her views are equally unenlightened. When Lydia rejects Jack's suit, arguing that her preference for Beverley has prompted an aversion for all other suitors, Mrs Malaprop's response is blunt: 'What business have you, Miss, with *preference* and *aversion*?'. Marital arrangements are the domain of parents and guardians, and questions of love and compatibility have no place.

However, Lydia's romantic attitude is also ridiculed. Her knowledge of love has been gleaned from the romantic novels she borrows in such vast quantities from those very 'circulating libraries' on which Sir Anthony pours such scorn. When we first see Lydia, she is already estranged from her beloved Ensign Beverley. Fearing never to taste the delights of a lovers' quarrel (of which she has no doubt read), she has sent herself an 'anonymous' letter claiming that he has been unfaithful and, confronting him with it, has put herself in a 'violent passion' and has banished him from her presence.

This is just one facet of Lydia's generally contrary nature. As well as seeking 'disinterested love', she welcomes the attentions of the impecunious Beverley precisely in order to 'incense' her aunt. Since this would entail losing the greater part of her fortune, Lydia's actions constitute the epitome of self-defeating youthful rebellion. Upon learning that Beverley is in reality the eminently eligible Jack Absolute, she rejects him, furious because she has been duped and because her plan to marry into poverty is now thwarted. Lydia's vision of marriage, then, is naive and adolescent and, although her desire for a romantically poor match might be greeted with some sympathy today, an eighteenth century audience would have displayed no such understanding. In an age that valued prudence, Lydia's wilful rejection of the advantages of her birth would have seemed mere foolishness.

The character of Lydia is paralleled in the subplot by that of Faulkland. Faulkland, we discover, once saved Julia from drowning, In response she swore her devotion to him, while her late father offered Faulkland Julia's hand in marriage. But Faulkland is an over-sensitive lover, beset by uncertainty and constantly finding improbable reasons for doubting Julia's love. Before the play opens,

we learn, Julia has been visiting relations in the country and
Faulkland has, for no apparent reason, been racked by fears for her
health. On discovering that she is well and has been singing and
dancing, he marvels that she could remain in such high spirits when
parted from him and, fearing therefore that her love is insincere,
once again sinks comically into despair.

The subplot of Julia and Faulkland is not fully integrated into the
main action of the play, but echoes it thematically. Just as Lydia
seeks a match based on love alone, Faulkland fears that Julia's
apparent devotion is merely a mask for her gratitude and sense of
duty to her dead father. Both seek an ideal of disinterested love in an
age when marriage was often contracted solely to meet social and
financial obligations. In all other ways, however, these two characters
are presented quite differently. Lydia is lampooned as a foolish girl,
but, while Faulkland's constant self doubt may seem funny on the
modern stage, his character in the eighteenth century would have
appeared far more sympathetic. Although comic, his emotional
depth and sensitivity mark him out as a 'man of sensibility', that
embodiment of refinement and deep feeling much loved by Georgian
audiences, and Faulkland proved one of the play's most popular
characters even from the first, badly received performance.

The plot, then, is centred upon conflicting attitudes towards
matrimony, for Lydia's and Faulkland's desire for a contract of the
heart is entirely at odds with Sir Anthony's and Mrs Malaprop's
view. But comedy requires a happy conclusion, and this is effected by
Julia and Jack. Julia is patient and devoted, but she is also perceptive.
She is willing to put up with Faulkland's endless fault-finding and
even to follow him into exile because, as she explains to Lydia, his
behaviour is caused by his own lack of self esteem. Yet Julia is no
two-dimensional saint, for she is human enough to reject Faulkland
when he tests her sincerity once too often, and to forgive him when
he subsequently proves repentant. Julia combines sensibility with
good sense, and although she may appear rather too passive for
modern tastes, she embodies precisely those qualities felt proper for a
woman of the eighteenth century.

Jack Absolute is a character familiar from many English comedies, for the plays of the preceding two centuries frequently feature young lovers who, at odds with parents and figures of authority, must resort to disguise and trickery to win the maiden. Jack is given more asides than other characters, enabling the actor playing him to build a sense of intimacy with the audience, and as a result the audience becomes privy to his ploys, delighting in them even more. But he is never completely in control of events, and the several reversals of fortune that beset Jack make him a more sympathetic figure. Jack's love for Lydia is sincere, as displayed by the patience with which he bears her foibles. Yet he proves eminently aware of life's practicalities, reacting to Faulkland's suggestion that they elope with 'What, and lose two thirds of her fortune?'. Jack is sensible and realistic, qualities admired in Sheridan's England, and it is by his contrivance that he and Lydia are finally able to marry with their finances intact, creating a union that is both emotionally and financially secure. In the play's resolution 'sensible' love consists of romance tempered by prudence and a proper appreciation of life's realities, that balance of the private and public so central to eighteenth century sensibilities.

The Georgian Stage

Theatre in eighteenth-century England was varied but humour and frivolity dominated. Comedy was half as popular again as tragedy in the London repertoires, with Shakespeare by far the most performed playwright. Farce and, particularly, pantomime were more popular still, and it is during this century that the ballad drama (like Sheridan's own *The Duenna*) develops as a significant form. However, the audience of a play such as *The Rivals* would seldom have been treated to only one entertainment. The plays were often preceded by music, pageants and processions, the interludes were filled with songs and comic dances, and, after the play ended, the evening was often capped with a short farce or burlesque.

While audiences for Georgian drama were mixed, they were differentiated by the seating arrangements. The aristocracy and gentry occupied expensive front and side boxes, working-class spectators sat in the cheap seats of the upper gallery, while the lower gallery and pit were the preserve of the professional, trade and middle-class spectators. The pit was also favoured by the 'critics': not only professional journalists but those of the audience who took upon themselves the right to comment on the performance as it took place, shouting approval or, more often, disapproval. Such behaviour from an audience may seem astonishing today; we are accustomed to sitting in our seats, still, in darkness, and maintaining a respectful silence. But the auditorium of the eighteenth century theatre was as brightly lit as the stage, and almost as active. The original audience of *The Rivals* would have felt free to talk, eat, walk around and greet their friends, and to make their opinion of the play loudly known. Raucous behaviour was the norm and the histories of the Covent Garden and Drury Lane theatres are filled with stories of interrupted performances and even riots.

As for the playing area itself, the stage of eighteenth century England was not so very different from the modern proscenium arch. It consisted of a deeply recessed upstage area (farthest from the audience) and a forestage that thrust some distance into the auditorium; although as the century progressed, the forestage was made shorter to accommodate more seats. Theatres came to employ basic stage machinery such as stage traps and 'cuts' (long, thin traps running across the stage, through which pieces of painted scenery, for instance, could be made to pop up). In the upstage area a system of lateral floor grooves allowed tiers of painted scenes to be slid onstage, creating the illusion of receding perspective. The art of scenic design was thriving in Sheridan's time and, although standard sets were used for most productions, noted scene painters would be employed to make new and special pieces. But, as we have noted, the sets provided merely the backdrop for the action, as the acting itself took place on the forestage. With the progressive shortening of the forestage the actors were gradually driven back into the scenic area, further from the audience, as in many modern theatres.

Acting itself varied widely over the century, but by 1775 the most favoured style was exemplified by David Garrick. Previously performances had displayed little movement and had concentrated instead on fine diction and dignified or comic posture. From his debut performance in 1741 Garrick introduced a heightened emotionalism to the London stage. His performances were marked by physicality – vigorous movement, emphatic gesture – and by sudden and dramatic changes in mood and register. This heightened activity was appropriate to the expression of eighteenth century 'sensibility', although its popularity is also linked, perhaps, to the progressive shortening of the forestage and the greater distance between stage and many members of the audience that resulted from it. Whatever the case, Garrick came to influence a whole generation of English actors, and his style of performance dominated the stage for which *The Rivals* was written.

Colin Counsell,
London, 1994

For Further Reading

Stanley Ayling's *A Portrait of Sheridan* is a detailed and interesting biography of the playwright. John Loftis's *Sheridan and the Drama of Georgian England* (Basil Blackwell, 1976) provides a good analysis of *The Rivals*, while Richard W. Bevis's *English Drama: Restoration and Eighteenth Century, 1660-1789* (Longman, 1988) is a modern and comprehensive look at this period of drama as a whole. For a general introduction to eighteenth century theatre, there is no more accessible text than Volume VI of *The Revels History of Drama in English* (Methuen, 1975). D. J. Palmer's (ed.) *Comedy: Developments in Criticism* in Macmillan's Casebook series contains key extracts from the debate on comedy that was taking place in Sheridan's time.

Sheridan: Key Dates

1751	4 November, Sheridan christened at St Mary's Church, Dublin (precise date of birth unknown).
1773	13 April, married Elizabeth Linley.
1775	17 January, first production of *The Rivals* at Covent Garden Theatre, scorned by critics.
1775	28 January, production of revised version of *The Rivals* at Covent Garden Theatre, a success.
1776	21 September, having bought shares in Drury Lane Theatre, becomes Principal Manager.
1780	12 September, elected Member of Parliament for Stafford.
1809	24 February, Drury Lane Theatre destroyed by fire.
1812	Autumn, losses parliamentary seat.
1816	7 July, Sheridan dies. 13 July, buried in Poet's Corner, Westminster Abbey.

THE RIVALS

Preface

A preface to a play seems generally to be considered as a kind of closet-prologue, in which – if his piece has been successful – the author solicits that indulgence from the reader which he had before experienced from the audience: but as the scope and immediate object of a play is to please a mixed assembly in the representation (whose judgement in the theatre at least is decisive) its degree of reputation is usually as determined as public, before it can be prepared for the cooler tribunal of the study. Thus any further solicitude on the part of the writer becomes unnecessary at least, if not an intrusion: and if the piece has been condemned in the performance, I fear an address to the closet, like an appeal to posterity, is constantly regarded as the procrastination of a suit, from a consciousness of the weakness of the cause. From these considerations, the following comedy would certainly have been submitted to the reader, without any further introduction than what it had in the representation, but that its success has probably been founded on a circumstance which the author is informed has not before attended a theatrical trial, and which consequently ought not to pass unnoticed.

I need scarcely add, that the circumstance alluded to, was the withdrawing of the piece, to remove those imperfections in the first representation which were too obvious to escape reprehension, and too numerous to admit of a hasty correction. There are few writers, I believe, who, even in the fullest consciousness of error, do not wish to palliate the faults which they acknowledge- and, however trifling the performance, to second their confession of its deficiencies, by whatever plea seems least disgraceful to their ability. In the present instance, it cannot be said to amount either to candour or modesty in me, to acknowledge an extreme inexperience and want of judgement on matters, in which, without guidance from practice, or spur from success, a young man should scarcely boast of being an adept. If it be said, that under such disadvantages no one should attempt to write a play – I must beg leave to dissent from the position, while the first point of experience that I have gained on the subject is, a knowledge of the candour and judgement with which an impartial public distinguishes between the errors of inexperience and incapacity, and the indulgence which it shows even to a disposition to remedy the defects of either.

It were unnecessary to enter into any farther extenuation of what was thought exceptionable in this play, but that it has been said, that the managers should have prevented some of the defects before its appearance to the public – and in particular the uncommon length of the piece as represented the first night. It were an ill return for the most liberal and gentlemanly conduct on their side, to suffer any censure to rest where none was deserved. Hurry in writing has long been exploded as an excuse for an author; however, in the dramatic line, it may happen, that both an author and a manager may wish to fill a chasm in the entertainment of the public with a hastiness not altogether culpable. The season was advanced when I first put the play into Mr Harris's hand: it was at that time at least double the length of any acting comedy. I profited by his judgement and experience in the curtailing of it – till, I believe, his feeling for the vanity of a young author got the better of his desire for correctness, and he left many excrescences remaining, because he had assisted in pruning so many more. Hence, though I was not uninformed that the acts were still too long, I flattered myself that, after the first trial, I might with safer judgement proceed to remove what should appear to have been most dissatisfactory. Many other errors there were, which might in part have arisen from my being by no means conversant with plays in general, either in reading or at the theatre. Yet I own that, in one respect, I did not regret my ignorance: for as my first wish in attempting a play, was to avoid every appearance of plagiary, I thought I should stand a better chance of effecting this from being in a walk which I had not frequented, and where consequently the progress of invention was less likely to be interrupted by starts of recollection: for on subjects on which the mind has been much informed, invention is slow of exerting itself. Faded ideas float in the fancy like half-forgotten dreams; and the imagination in its fullest enjoyments becomes suspicious of its offspring, and doubts whether it has created or adopted .

With regard to some particular passages which on the first night's representation seemed generally disliked, I confess, that if I felt any emotion of surprise at the disapprobation, it was not that they were disapproved of, but that I had not before perceived that they deserved it. As some part of the attack on the piece was begun too early to pass for the sentence of judgement, which is ever tardy in condemning, it has been suggested to me, that much of the disapprobation must have arisen from virulence of malice, rather than severity of criticism: but as I was more apprehensive of there being just grounds to excite the latter, than conscious of having deserved the former, I continue not to believe that probable, which I am sure must have been unprovoked. However, if it was so, and I could even mark the quarter from whence it came, it would be ungenerous to retort; for no passion suffers more than malice from disappointment. For my own part, I see no reason why the author of a play should not regard a first night's audience, as a candid and judicious friend attending, in behalf of the public, at his last rehearsal. If he can dispense with flattery, he is sure at least of sincerity, and even though the annotation be rude, he may rely upon the justness of the comment. Considered in this light, that audience, whose *fiat* is essential to the poet's claim, whether his object be fame or profit, has surely a right to expect some deference to its opinion, from principles of politeness at least, if not from gratitude.

As for the little puny critics, who scatter their peevish strictures in private circles, and scribble at every author who has the eminence of being unconnected with them, as they are usually spleen-swollen from a vain idea of increasing their consequence, there will always be found a petulance and illiberality in their remarks, which should place them as far beneath the notice of a gentleman, as their original dullness had sunk them from the level of the most unsuccessful author.

It is not without pleasure that I catch at an opportunity of justifying myself from the charge of intending any national reflection in the character of Sir Lucius O'Trigger. If any gentlemen opposed the piece from that idea, I thank them sincerely for their opposition; and if the condemnation of this comedy (however misconceived the provocation) could have added one spark to the decaying flame of national attachment to the country supposed to be reflected on, I should have been happy in its fate; and might with truth have boasted, that it had done more real service in its failure, than the successful morality of a thousand stage-novels will ever effect.

It is usual, I believe, to thank the performers in a new play, for the exertion of their several abilities. But where (as in this instance) their merit has been so striking and uncontroverted, as to call for the warmest and truest applause from a number of judicious audiences, the poet's after-praise comes like the feeble acclamation of a child to close the shouts of a multitude. The conduct, however, of the principals in a theatre cannot be so apparent to the public. I think it therefore but justice to declare, that from this theatre (the only one I can speak of from experience) those writers who wish to try the dramatic line, will meet with that candour and liberal attention, which are generally allowed to be better calculated to lead genius into excellence, than either the precepts of judgement, or the guidance of experience.   THE AUTHOR

Prologue

By the Author

Spoken by Mr Woodward and Mr Quick

Enter SERJEANT AT LAW, *and* ATTORNEY *following, and giving a paper.*

SERJEANT. What's here – a vile cramp hand! I cannot see
   Without my spectacles.

ATTORNEY.   He means his fee.
   Nay, Mr Serjeant, good Sir, try again.

   Gives money.

SERJEANT. The scrawl improves – (*More money is given.*)
     O come, 'tis pretty plain.
   Hey! how's this? Dibble! sure it cannot be!
   A poet's brief! A poet and a fee!

ATTORNEY. Yea Sir!—though you without reward, I know
   Would gladly plead the muses' cause –

SERJEANT.   So – So !

ATTORNEY. And if the fee offends – your wrath should fall
   On me –

SERJEANT. Dear Dibble no offence at all –

ATTORNEY. Some sons of Phoebus in the courts we meet,

SERJEANT. And fifty sons of Phoebus in the Fleet!

ATTORNEY. Nor pleads he worse, who with a decent sprig
   Of bays adorns his legal waste of wig.

SERJEANT. Full-bottomed heroes thus, on signs, unfurl

A leaf of laurel – in a grove of curl!
Yet tell your client, that, in adverse days,
This wig is warmer than a bush of bays.

ATTORNEY. Do you then, Sir, my client's place supply,
Profuse of robe, and prodigal of tie –
Do you, with all those blushing powers of face,
And wonted bashful hesitating grace,
Rise in the court, and flourish on the case.

Exit.

SERJEANT. For practice then suppose – this brief will show it –
Me, Serjeant Woodward, counsel for the poet.
Used to the ground – I know 'tis hard to deal
With this dread court from whence there's no appeal;
No tricking here, to blunt the edge of law,
Or, damned in equity, escape by flaw:
But judgement given, your sentence must remain;
No writ of error lies to Drury Lane!
Yet when so kind you seem, 'tis past dispute
We gain some favour, if not costs of suit.
No spleen is here! I see no hoarded fury;
I think I never faced a milder jury!
Sad else our plight! – where frowns are transportation,
A hiss the gallows, and a groan, damnation!
But such the public candour, without fear
My client waives all right of challenge here.
No newsman from our session is dismissed,
Nor wit nor critic we scratch off the list;
His faults can never hurt another's ease,
His crime at worst – a bad attempt to please:
Thus, all respecting, he appeals to all,
And by the general voice will stand or fall.

Prologue

By the Author

Spoken on the tenth night, by Mrs Bulkley

Granted our cause, our suit and trial o'er,
The worthy Serjeant need appear no more:
In pleasing I a different client choose
He served the poet – I would serve the muse:
Like him, I'll try to merit your applause,
A female counsel in a female's cause.
Look on this form – where humour quaint and sly
Dimples the cheek, and points the beaming eye;
Where gay invention seems to boast its wiles
In amorous hint, and half-triumphant smiles;
While her light masks or covers satire's strokes,
All hide the conscious blush, her wit provokes.
Look on her well – does she seem formed to teach?
Should you expect to hear this lady – preach?
Is grey experience suited to her youth?
Do solemn sentiments become that mouth?
Bid her be grave, those lips should rebel prove
To every theme that slanders mirth or love.
Yet thus adorned with every graceful art
To charm the fancy and yet reach the heart
Must we displace her? And instead advance
The goddess of the woeful countenance –
The sentimental muse! Her emblems view
The *Pilgrim's Progress*, and a sprig of rue!
View her – too chaste to look like flesh and blood –
Primly portrayed on emblematic wood!
Thus fixed in usurpation should she stand
She'll snatch the dagger from her sister's hand:
And having made her votaries weep a flood

Good heaven! she'll end her comedies in blood –
Bid Harry Woodward break poor Dunstall's crown!
Imprison Quick – and knock Ned Shuter down;
While sad Barsanti – weeping o'er the scene,
Shall stab herself – or poison Mrs Green.
Such dire encroachments to prevent in time,
Demands the critic's voice – the poet's rhyme.
Can our light scenes add strength to holy laws!
Such puny patronage but hurts the cause:
Fair virtue scorns our feeble aid to ask;
And moral truth disdains the trickster's mask.
For here their favourite stands, whose brow – severe
And sad – claims youth's respect, and pity's tear;
Who – when oppressed by foes her worth creates –
Can point a poignard at the guilt she hates.

Dramatis Personae

Men

SIR ANTHONY ABSOLUTE
CAPTAIN ABSOLUTE
FAULKLAND
ACRES
SIR LUCIUS O TRIGGER
FAG
DAVID
COACHMAN
[ERRAND BOY
SERVANTS]

Women

MRS MALAPROP
LYDIA LANGUISH
JULIA
LUCY
[MAID]

Scene, Bath

Time of action, within one day

Act I, Scene i

A street in Bath

COACHMAN *crosses the stage. Enter* FAG, *looking after him.*

FAG. What! – Thomas! – Sure 'tis he? – What! – Thomas! – Thomas!

COACHMAN. Hey! – Odds life! Mr Fag! – give us your hand, my old fellow-servant.

FAG. Excuse my glove, Thomas: I'm devilish glad to see you, my lad: why, my prince of charioteers, you look as hearty! – but who the deuce thought of seeing you in Bath!

COACHMAN. Sure, Master, Madam Julia, Harry, Mrs Kate, and the postillion be all come!

FAG. Indeed!

COACHMAN. Aye! Master thought another fit of the gout was coming to make him a visit: so he'd a mind to gi't the slip, and whip we were all off at an hour's warning.

FAG. Aye, aye! hasty in everything, or it would not be Sir Anthony Absolute!

COACHMAN. But tell us, Mr Fag, how does young Master? Odd! Sir Anthony will stare to see the Captain here!

FAG. I do not serve Captain Absolute now –

COACHMAN. Why sure!

FAG. At present I am employed by Ensign Beverley.

COACHMAN. I doubt, Mr Fag, you ha'n't changed for the better.

FAG. I have not changed, Thomas.

COACHMAN. No! why didn't you say you had left young Master?

FAG. No – well, honest Thomas, I must puzzle you no farther: briefly then – Captain Absolute and Ensign Beverley are one and the same person.

COACHMAN. The devil they are!

FAG. So it is indeed, Thomas; and the *Ensign* half of my master being on guard at present – the *Captain* has nothing to do with me.

COACHMAN. So, so! – what, this is some freak, I warrant! Do, tell us, Mr Fag, the meaning o't – you know I ha' trusted you.

FAG. You'll be secret, Thomas.

COACHMAN. As a coach-horse.

FAG. Why then the cause of all this is – L, O, V, E, – love,Thomas, who (as you may get read to you) has been a masquerader ever since the days of Jupiter.

COACHMAN. Aye, aye; I guessed there was a lady in the case: but pray, why does your master pass only for Ensign? now if he had shammed General indeed –

FAG. Ah! Thomas, there lies the mystery o'the matter. Harkee, Thomas, my master is in love with a lady of a very singular taste: a lady who likes him better as a half-pay Ensign than if she knew he was son and heir to Sir Anthony Absolute, a baronet with three thousand a year!

COACHMAN. That is an odd taste indeed! – but has she got the stuff, Mr Fag; is she rich, hey?

FAG. Rich! – why, I believe she owns half the stocks! Zounds! Thomas, she could pay the national debt as easy as I could my washerwoman! She has a lap-dog that eats out of gold – she feeds her parrot with small pearls – and all her thread-papers are made of bank-notes!

COACHMAN. Bravo! – faith! – odd! I warrant she has a set of thousands at least: but does she draw kindly with the Captain?

FAG. As fond as pigeons.

COACHMAN. May one hear her name?

FAG. Miss Lydia Languish – but there is an old tough aunt in the way; though by the bye she has never seen my master – for he got acquainted with Miss while on a visit in Gloucestershire.

COACHMAN. Well – I wish they were once harnessed together in matrimony. But pray, Mr Fag, what kind of a place is this Bath? I ha' heard a deal of it – here's a mort o' merrymaking – hey?

FAG. Pretty well, Thomas, pretty well – 'tis a good lounge. In the morning we go to the pump-room (though neither my master nor I drink the waters); after breakfast we saunter on the parades or play a game at billiards; at night we dance: but damn the place, I'm tired of it: their regular hours stupefy me – not a fiddle nor a card after eleven! – however Mr Faulkland's gentleman and I keep it up a little in private parties, I'll introduce you there Thomas – you'll like him much.

COACHMAN. Sure I know Mr Du-Peigne – you know his master is to marry Madam Julia.

FAG. I had forgot. But Thomas you must polish a little – indeed you must: here now – this wig! – what the devil do you do with a wig, Thomas? None of the London whips of any degree of ton wear wigs now.

COACHMAN. More's the pity! more's the pity, I say. Odds life! when I heard how the lawyers and doctors had took to their own hair, I thought how 'twould go next – odd rabbit it! when the fashion had got foot on the Bar, I guessed 'twould mount to the Box! – but 'tis all out of character, believe me, Mr Fag: and lookee, I'll never gi' up mine – the lawyers and doctors may do as they will.

FAG. Well, Thomas, we'll not quarrel about that.

COACHMAN. Why, bless you, the gentlemen of they professions ben't all of a mind – for in our village now tho'ff Jack Gauge the exciseman has ta'en to his carrots, there's little Duck the farrier swears he'll never forsake his bob, though all the college should appear with their own heads!

FAG. Indeed! well said Dick! but hold – mark! mark! Thomas.

COACHMAN. Zooks! 'tis the Captain – is that the lady with him?

FAG. No! no! that is Madam Lucy – my master's mistress's maid. They lodge at that house – but I must after him to tell him the news.

COACHMAN. Odd! he's giving her money! – well, Mr Fag –

FAG. Goodbye, Thomas – I have an appointment in Gyde's Porch this evening at eight; meet me there, and we'll make a little party.

Exeunt severally.

Scene ii

A dressing-room in MRS MALAPROP's *lodgings.* LYDIA *sitting on a sofa with a book in her hand.* LUCY, *as just returned from a message*

LUCY. Indeed, Ma'am, I transferred half the town in search of it: I don't believe there's a circulating library in Bath I ha'n't been at.

LYDIA. And could not you get *The Reward of Constancy?*

LUCY. No, indeed, Ma'am.

LYDIA. Nor *The Fatal Connection?*

LUCY. No, indeed, Ma'am.

LYDIA. Nor *The Mistakes of the Heart?*

LUCY. Ma'am, as ill-luck would have it, Mr Bull said Miss Sukey Saunter had just fetched it away.

LYDIA. Heigh-ho! – did you inquire for *The Delicate Distress?*

LUCY. Or *The Memoirs of Lady Woodford?* Yes indeed, Ma'am. I asked everywhere for it; and I might have brought it from Mr Frederick's, but Lady Slattern Lounger, who had just sent it home, had so soiled and dog's-eared it, it wa'n't fit for a Christian to read.

LYDIA. Heigh-ho! – yes, I always know when Lady Slattern has been before me. She has a most observing thumb – and I believe cherishes her nails for the convenience of making marginal notes. Well, child, what *have* you brought me?

LUCY. Oh! here Ma'am. (*Taking books from under her cloak, and from her pockets.*) This is *The Gordian Knot* – and this *Peregrine Pickle.* Here are *The Tears of Sensibility,* and *Humphrey Clinker.* This is *The Memoirs of a Lady of Quality, written by herself* – and here the second volume of *The Sentimental Journey.*

LYDIA. Heigh-ho! – what are those books by the glass?

LUCY. The great one is only *The Whole Duty of Man* – where I press a few blondes, Ma'am.

LYDIA. Very well – give me the *sal volatile.*

LUCY. Is it in a blue cover, Ma'am?

LYDIA. My smelling bottle, you simpleton!

LUCY. Oh, the drops! – here Ma'am.

LYDIA. Hold! – here's someone coming – quick, see who it is.

Exit LUCY.

Surely I heard my cousin Julia's voice!

[*Enter*] LUCY.

LUCY Lud! Ma'am, here is Miss Melville.

LYDIA. Is it possible!

Enter JULIA, [*exit* LUCY.]

LYDIA. My dearest Julia, how delighted am I! (*Embrace.*) How unexpected was this happiness!

JULIA. True, Lydia – and our pleasure is the greater; but what has been the matter? You were denied to me at first!

LYDIA. Ah! Julia, I have a thousand things to tell you! But first inform me, what has conjured you to Bath? Is Sir Anthony here?

JULIA. He is – we are arrived within this hour – and I suppose he will be here to wait on Mrs Malaprop as soon as he is dressed.

LYDIA. Then before we are interrupted, let me impart to you some of my distress! I know your gentle nature will sympathise with me, though your prudence may condemn me! My letters have informed you of my whole connection with Beverley – but I have lost him, Julia! – my aunt has discovered our intercourse by a note she intercepted, and has confined me ever since! – Yet, would you believe it? she has fallen absolutely in love with a tall Irish baronet she met one night since we have been here, at Lady Macshuffle's rout.

JULIA. You jest, Lydia!

LYDIA. No, upon my word. She really carries on a kind of correspondence with him, under a feigned name though, till she chooses to be known to him – but it is a *Delia* or a *Celia*, I assure you.

JULIA. Then, surely, she is now more indulgent to her niece.

LYDIA. Quite the contrary. Since she has discovered her own frailty, she is become more suspicious of mine. Then I must inform you of another plague! That odious Acres is to be in Bath today; so that I protest I shall be teased out of all spirits!

JULIA. Come, come, Lydia, hope the best – Sir Anthony shall use his interest with Mrs Malaprop.

LYDIA. But you have not heard the worst. Unfortunately I had quarrelled with my poor Beverley, just before my aunt made the discovery, and I have not seen him since, to make it up.

JULIA. What was his offence?

LYDIA. Nothing at all! But, I don't know how it was, as often as we had been together, we had never had a quarrel! And, somehow I was afraid he would never give me an opportunity. So, last Thursday, I wrote a letter to myself, to inform myself that Beverley was at that time paying his addresses to another woman. I signed it *your Friend unknown,* showed it to Beverley, charged him with his falsehood, put myself in a violent passion, and vowed I'd never see him more.

JULIA. And you let him depart so, and have not seen him since?

LYDIA. 'Twas the next day my aunt found the matter out. I intended only to have teased him three days and a half, and now I've lost him for ever.

JULIA. If he is as deserving and sincere as you have represented him to me, he will never give you up so. Yet consider, Lydia, you tell me he is but an ensign, and you have thirty thousand pounds!

LYDIA. But you know I lose most of my fortune, if I marry without my aunt's consent, till of age; and that is what I have determined to do, ever since I knew the penalty. Nor could I love the man, who would wish to wait a day for the alternative.

JULIA. Nay, this is caprice!

LYDIA. What, does Julia tax me with caprice? I thought her lover Faulkland had inured her to it.

JULIA. I do not love even *his* faults.

LYDIA. But apropos – you have sent to him, I suppose?

JULIA. Not yet, upon my word – nor has he the least idea of my being in Bath. Sir Anthony's resolution was so sudden, I could not inform him of it.

LYDIA. Well, Julia, you are your own mistress (though under the protection of Sir Anthony), yet have you, for this long year, been a slave to the caprice, the whim, the jealousy of this ungrateful Faulkland, who will ever delay assuming the right of a husband, while you suffer him to be equally imperious as a lover.

JULIA. Nay you are wrong entirely. We were contracted before my fathers death. *That*, and some consequent embarrassments, have delayed what I know to be my Faulkland's most ardent wish. He is too generous to trifle on such a point. And for his character, you wrong him there too – no, Lydia, he is too proud, too noble to be jealous; if he is captious, 'tis without dissembling, if fretful, without rudeness. Unused to the fopperies of love, he is negligent of the little duties expected from a lover – but being unhackneyed in the passion, his affection is ardent and sincere; and as it engrosses his whole soul, he expects every thought and emotion of his mistress to move in unison with his. Yet, though his pride calls for this full return – his humility makes him undervalue those qualities in him, which would entitle him to it; and not feeling why he should be loved to the degree he wishes, he still suspects that he is not loved enough. This temper, I must own, has cost me many unhappy hours; but I have learned to think myself his debtor, for those imperfections which arise from the ardour of his attachment.

LYDIA. Well, I cannot blame you for defending him. But tell me candidly, Julia, had he never saved your life, do you think you should have been attached to him as you are? Believe me, the rude blast that overset your boat was a prosperous gale of love to him.

JULIA. Gratitude may have strengthened my attachment to Mr Faulkland, but I loved him before he had preserved me; yet surely that alone were an obligation sufficient –

LYDIA. Obligation! Why a water-spaniel would have done as much! Well, I should never think of giving my heart to a man because he could swim!

JULIA. Come, Lydia, you are too inconsiderate.

LYDIA. Nay, I do but jest – what's here?

Enter LUCY *in a hurry*.

LUCY. O Ma'am, here is Sir Anthony Absolute just come home with your aunt.

LYDIA. They'll not come here – Lucy, do you watch.

Exit LUCY.

JULIA. Yet I must go – Sir Anthony does not know I am here, and if we meet, he'll detain me, to show me the town. I'll take another opportunity of paying my respects to Mrs Malaprop, when she shall treat me, as long as she chooses, with her select words so ingeniously *misapplied*, without being *mispronounced*.

[*Enter*] LUCY.

LUCY. O Lud! Ma'am, they are both coming upstairs.

LYDIA. Well, I'll not detain you coz – adieu, my dear Julia, I'm sure you are in haste to send to Faulkland. There – through my room you'll find another staircase.

JULIA. Adieu. (*Embrace.*)

Exit JULIA.

LYDIA. Here, my dear Lucy, hide these books – quick, quick – fling *Peregrine Pickle* under the toilet – throw *Roderick Random* into the closet – put *The Innocent Adultery* into *The Whole Duty of Man* – thrust *Lord Aimworth* under the sofa – cram Ovid behind the bolster – there – put *The Man of Feeling* into your pocket so, so, now lay *Mrs Chapone* in sight, and leave Fordyce's *Sermons* open on the table.

LUCY. O burn it, Ma'am, the hairdresser has torn away as far as 'Proper Pride'.

LYDIA. Never mind – open at 'Sobriety' – fling me Lord Chesterfield's *Letters*. Now for 'em.

[*Exit* LUCY.] *Enter* MRS MALAPROP *and* SIR ANTHONY ABSOLUTE.

MRS MALAPROP. There, Sir Anthony, there sits the deliberate simpleton, who wants to disgrace her family, and lavish herself on a fellow not worth a shilling!

LYDIA. Madam, I thought you once –

MRS MALAPROP. You thought, Miss! I don't know any business you have to think at all – thought does not become a young woman; the point we would request of you is, that you will promise to forget this fellow – to illiterate him, I say, quite from your memory.

LYDIA. Ah! Madam! our memories are independent of our wills. It is not so easy to forget.

MRS MALAPROP. But I say it is, Miss; there is nothing on earth so easy as to *forget*, if a person chooses to set about it. I'm sure I have as much forgot your poor dear uncle as if he had never existed – and I thought it my duty so to do; and let me tell you, Lydia, these violent memories don't become a young woman.

SIR ANTHONY. Why sure she won't pretend to remember what she's ordered not! Aye, this comes of her reading!

LYDIA. What crime, Madam, have I committed to be treated thus?

MRS MALAPROP. Now don't attempt to extirpate yourself from the matter; you know I have proof controvertible of it. But tell me, will you promise to do as you're bid? Will you take a husband of your friend's choosing?

LYDIA. Madam, I must tell you plainly, that had I no preference for anyone else, the choice you have made would be my aversion.

MRS MALAPROP. What business have you, Miss, with *preference* and *aversion?* They don't become a young woman; and you ought to know, that as both always wear off, 'tis safest in matrimony to begin with a little aversion. I am sure I hated your poor dear uncle before marriage as if he'd been a blackamoor – and yet, Miss, you are sensible what a wife I made! – and when it pleased Heaven to release me from him, 'tis unknown what tears I shed! But suppose we were going to give you another choice, will you promise us to give up this Beverley?

LYDIA. Could I belie my thoughts so far, as to give that promise, my actions would certainly as far belie my words.

MRS MALAPROP. Take yourself to your room. You are fit company for nothing but your own ill-humours.

LYDIA. Willingly, Ma'am – I cannot change for the worse.

Exit LYDIA.

MRS MALAPROP. There's a little intricate hussy for you!

SIR ANTHONY. It is not to be wondered at, Ma'am – all this is the natural consequence of teaching girls to read. Had I a thousand daughters, by heaven! I'd as soon have them taught the black art as their alphabet!

MRS MALAPROP. Nay, nay, Sir Anthony, you are an absolute misanthropy!

SIR ANTHONY. In my way hither, Mrs Malaprop, I observed your niece's maid coming forth from a circulating library! She had a book in each hand – they were half-bound volumes, with marble covers! From that moment I guessed how full of duty I should see her mistress!

MRS MALAPROP. Those are vile places, indeed!

SIR ANTHONY. Madam, a circulating library in a town is as an ever-green tree of diabolical knowledge! It blossoms through the year! And depend on it, Mrs Malaprop, that they who are so fond of handling the leaves, will long for the fruit at last.

MRS MALAPROP. Well, but Sir Anthony, your wife, Lady Absolute, was fond of books.

SIR ANTHONY. Aye – and injury sufficient they were to her, Madam. But were I to choose another helpmate, the extent of her erudition should consist in her knowing her simple letters without their mischievous combinations; and the summit of her science be – her ability to count as far as twenty. The first, Mrs Malaprop, would enable her to work A.A. upon my linen, and the latter would be quite sufficient to prevent her giving me a shirt, No. 1 and a stock, No. 2.

MRS MALAPROP. Fie, fie, Sir Anthony, you surely speak laconically!

SIR ANTHONY. Why, Mrs Malaprop, in moderation, now, what would you have a woman know?

MRS MALAPROP. Observe me, Sir Anthony. I would by no means wish a daughter of mine to be a progeny of learning; I don't think so much learning becomes a young woman; for instance – I would never let her meddle with Greek, or Hebrew, or Algebra, or Simony, or Fluxions, or Paradoxes, or such inflammatory branches of learning – neither would it be necessary for her to handle any of your mathematical, astronomical, diabolical instruments. But, Sir Anthony, I would send her, at nine years old, to a boarding-school, in order to learn a little ingenuity and artifice. Then, Sir, she should have a supercilious knowledge in accounts; and as she grew up, I would have her instructed in geometry, that she might know something of the contagious countries; but above all, Sir Anthony, she should be mistress of orthodoxy, that she might not mis-spell, and mispronounce words so shamefully as girls usually do; and likewise that she might reprehend the true meaning of what she is saying. This, Sir Anthony, is what I would have a woman know; and I don't think there is a superstitious article in it.

SIR ANTHONY Well, well, Mrs Malaprop, I will dispute the point no further with you; though I must confess, that you are a truly moderate and polite arguer, for almost every third word you say is on my side of the question. But, Mrs Malaprop, to the more important point in debate – you say, you have no objection to my proposal.

MRS MALAPROP. None, I assure you. I am under no positive engagement with Mr Acres, and as Lydia is so obstinate against him, perhaps your son may have better success.

SIR ANTHONY. Well, Madam, I will write for the boy directly. He knows not a syllable of this yet, though I have for some time had the proposal in my head. He is at present with his regiment.

MRS MALAPROP. We have never seen your son, Sir Anthony; but I hope no objection on his side.

SIR ANTHONY. Objection! – let him object if he dare! No, no, Mrs Malaprop, Jack knows that the least demur puts me in a frenzy directly. My process was always very simple – in their younger days, 'twas 'Jack, do this' – if he demurred – I knocked him down – and if he grumbled at that – I always sent him out of the room.

MRS MALAPROP. Aye, and the properest way, o' my conscience! – nothing is so conciliating to young people as severity. Well, Sir Anthony, I shall give Mr Acres his discharge, and prepare Lydia to receive your son's invocations; and I hope you will represent her to the Captain as an object not altogether illegible.

SIR ANTHONY. Madam, I will handle the subject prudently. Well, I must leave you – and let me beg you, Mrs Malaprop, to enforce this matter roundly to the girl, take my advice – keep a tight hand – if she rejects the proposal clap her under lock and key: and if you were just to let the servants forget to bring her dinner for three or four days, you can't conceive how she'd come about!

Exit SIR ANTHONY.

MRS MALAPROP. Well, at any rate I shall be glad to get her from under my intuition. She has somehow discovered my partiality for Sir Lucius O'Trigger – sure, Lucy can't have betrayed me! No, the girl is such a simpleton, I should have made her confess it. Lucy! – Lucy! (*Calls.*) Had she been one of your artificial ones, I should never have trusted her.

Enter LUCY.

LUCY. Did you call, Ma'am?

MRS MALAPROP. Yes, girl. Did you see Sir Lucius while you was out?

LUCY. No, indeed, Ma'am, not a glimpse of him.

MRS MALAPROP. You are sure, Lucy, that you never mentioned –

LUCY. O gemini! I'd sooner cut my tongue out.

MRS MALAPROP. Well, don't let your simplicity be imposed on.

LUCY. No, Ma'am.

MRS MALAPROP. So, come to me presently, and I'll give you another letter to Sir Lucius; but mind Lucy – if ever you betray what you are entrusted with (unless it be other people's secrets to me) you forfeit my malevolence for ever: and your being a simpleton shall be no excuse for your locality.

Exit MRS MALAPROP.

LUCY. Ha! ha! ha! So, my dear *simplicity*, let me give you a little respite (*Altering her manner.*) let girls in my station be as fond as they please of appearing expert, and knowing in their trusts; commend me to a mask of silliness, and a pair of sharp eyes for my own interest under it! Let me see to what account I have turned my *simplicity* lately – (*Looks at a paper.*) *For abetting Miss Lydia Languish in a design of running away with an ensign – in money – sundry times – twelve pound twelve – gowns, five – hats, ruffles, caps, etc, etc. – numberless! From the said Ensign, within this last month, six guineas and a half* – about a quarter's pay! Item, *from Mrs Malaprop, for betraying the young people to her* – when I found matters were likely to be discovered – *two guineas, and a black paduasoy.* Item, *from Mr Acres, for carrying divers letters* – which I never delivered – *two guineas, and a pair of buckles.* Item, *from Sir Lucius O'Trigger – three crowns – two gold pocket-pieces – and a silver snuff-box!* – Well done, *simplicity!* – yet I was forced to make my Hibernian believe, that he was corresponding, not with the aunt, but with the niece: for, though not over rich, I found he had too much pride and delicacy to sacrifice the feelings of a gentleman to the necessities of his fortune.

Exit .

Act II, Scene i

CAPTAIN ABSOLUTE's *lodgings*. CAPTAIN ABSOLUTE
and FAG.

FAG. Sir, while I was there, Sir Anthony came in: I told him you had
sent me to inquire after his health, and to know if he was at
leisure to see you.

ABSOLUTE. And what did he say, on hearing I was at Bath?

FAG. Sir, in my life I never saw an elderly gentleman more
astonished! He started back two or three paces, rapped out a
dozen interjectural oaths, and asked, what the devil had brought
you here!

ABSOLUTE. Well, Sir, and what did you say?

FAG. Oh, I lied, Sir – I forget the precise lie, but you may depend
on't; he got no truth from me. Yet, with submission, for fear of
blunders in future, I should be glad to fix what *has* brought us to
Bath: in order that we may lie a little consistently. Sir Anthony's
servants were curious, Sir, very curious indeed.

ABSOLUTE. You have said nothing to them?

FAG. Oh, not a word, Sir – not a word. Mr Thomas, indeed, the
coachman (whom I take to be the discreetest of whips) –

ABSOLUTE. 'Sdeath! – you rascal! you have not trusted him!

FAG. Oh, *no,* Sir – no – no – not a syllable, upon my veracity! He
was, indeed, a little inquisitive; but I was sly, Sir devilish sly! My
master (said I) honest Thomas (you know, Sir, one says *honest*
to one's inferiors) is come to Bath to *recruit* – yes, Sir – I said, to
recruit – and whether for men, money, or constitution, you know,
Sir, is nothing to him, nor anyone else.

ABSOLUTE. Well – recruit will do – let it be so –

FAG. Oh, Sir, recruit will do surprisingly – indeed, to give the thing an air, I told Thomas, that your honour had already enlisted five disbanded chairmen, seven minority waiters, and thirteen billiard markers.

ABSOLUTE. You blockhead, never say more than is necessary.

FAG. I beg pardon, Sir – I beg pardon. But with submission, a lie is nothing unless one supports it. Sir, whenever I draw on my invention for a good current lie, I always forge *endorsements,* as well as the bill.

ABSOLUTE. Well, take care you don't hurt your credit, by offering too much security. Is Mr Faulkland returned?

FAG. He is above, Sir, changing his dress.

ABSOLUTE. Can you tell whether he has been informed of Sir Anthony's and Miss Melville's arrival?

FAG. I fancy not, Sir; he has seen no one since he came in, but his gentleman, who was with him at Bristol. I think, Sir, I hear Mr Faulkland coming down –

ABSOLUTE. Go, tell him I am here.

FAG. Yes, Sir – (*Going.*) I beg pardon, Sir, but should Sir Anthony call, you will do me the favour to remember, that we are *recruiting,* if you please.

ABSOLUTE. Well, well.

FAG. And in tenderness to my character, if your honour could bring in the chairmen and waiters, I shall esteem it as an obligation; for though I never scruple a lie to serve my master, yet it hurts one's conscience, to be found out. (*Exit.*)

ABSOLUTE. Now for my whimsical friend – if he does not know that his mistress is here, I'll tease him a little before I tell him –

Enter FAULKLAND.

Faulkland, you're welcome to Bath again; you are punctual in your return.

FAULKLAND. Yes; I had nothing to detain me, when I had finished the business I went on. Well, what news since I left you? How stand matters between you and Lydia?

ABSOLUTE. Faith, much as they were; I have not seen her since our quarrel, however I expect to be recalled every hour.

FAULKLAND. Why don't you persuade her to go off with you at once?

ABSOLUTE. What, and lose two thirds of her fortune? You forget that my friend. No, no, I could have brought her to that long ago.

FAULKLAND. Nay then, you trifle too long – if you are sure of *her*, write to the aunt in your own character, and write to Sir Anthony for his consent.

ABSOLUTE. Softly, softly, for though I am convinced my little Lydia would elope with me as Ensign Beverley, yet am I by no means certain that she would take me with the impediment of our friends' consent, a regular humdrum wedding, and the reversion of a good fortune on my side; no, no, I must prepare her gradually for the discovery, and make myself necessary to her, before I risk it. Well, but Faulkland, you'll dine with us today at the hotel?

FAULKLAND. Indeed I cannot: I am not in spirits to be of such a party.

ABSOLUTE. By heavens! I shall forswear your company. You are the most teasing, captious, incorrigible lover! Do love like a man.

FAULKLAND. I own I am unfit for company.

ABSOLUTE. Am not *I* a lover; aye, and a romantic one too? Yet do I carry everywhere with me such a confounded farrago of doubts, fears, hopes, wishes, and all the flimsy furniture of a country miss's brain!

FAULKLAND. Ah! Jack, your heart and soul are not, like mine, fixed immutably on one only object. You throw for a large stake, but losing – you could stake, and throw again: but I have set my sum of happiness on this cast, and not to succeed, were to be stripped of all.

ABSOLUTE. But for heaven's sake! What grounds for apprehension can your whimsical brain conjure up at present?

FAULKLAND. What grounds for apprehension did you say? Heavens! are there not a thousand! I fear for her spirits – her health – her life. My absence may fret her; her anxiety for my return, her fears for me, may oppress her gentle temper. And for her health, does not every hour bring me cause to be alarmed? If it rains, some shower may even then have chilled her delicate frame! If the wind be keen, some rude blast may have affected her! The heat of noon, the dews of the evening, may endanger the life of her, for whom only I value mine. O Jack, when delicate and feeling souls are separated, there is not a feature in the sky, not a movement of the elements, not an aspiration of the breeze, but hints some cause for a lover's apprehension!

ABSOLUTE. Aye, but we may choose whether we will take the hint or not. So then, Faulkland, if you were convinced that Julia were well and in spirits, you would be entirely content?

FAULKLAND. I should be happy beyond measure – I am anxious only for that.

ABSOLUTE. Then to cure your anxiety at once – Miss Melville is in perfect health, and is at this moment in Bath.

FAULKLAND. Nay Jack – don't trifle with me.

ABSOLUTE. She is arrived here with my father within this hour.

FAULKLAND. Can you be serious?

ABSOLUTE. I thought you knew Sir Anthony better than to be surprised at a sudden whim of this kind. Seriously then, it is as I tell you – upon my honour.

FAULKLAND. My dear friend! Hollo, Du-Peigne! my hat – my dear Jack – now nothing on earth can give me a moment's uneasiness.

Enter FAG.

FAG. Sir, Mr Acres just arrived is below.

ABSOLUTE. Stay, Faulkland, this Acres lives within a mile of Sir Anthony, and he shall tell you how your mistress has been ever since you left her. Fag, show the gentleman up.

Exit FAG.

FAULKLAND. What, is he much acquainted in the family?

ABSOLUTE. Oh, very intimate: I insist on your not going: besides, his character will divert you.

FAULKLAND. Well, I should like to ask him a few questions.

ABSOLUTE. He is likewise a rival of mine – that is of my other self's, for he does not think his friend Captain Absolute ever saw the lady in question – and it is ridiculous enough to hear him complain to me of one Beverley, a concealed skulking rival, who –

FAULKLAND. Hush! He's here.

Enter ACRES.

ACRES. Hah! my dear friend, noble captain, and honest Jack, how do'st thou? Just arrived faith, as you see. [*To* FAULKLAND.] Sir, your humble servant. – Warm work on the roads Jack – odds whips and wheels, I've travelled like a comet, with a tail of dust all the way as long as the Mall.

ABSOLUTE. Ah! Bob, you are indeed an eccentric planet, but we know your attraction hither – give me leave to introduce Mr Faulkland to you; Mr Faulkland, Mr Acres.

ACRES. Sir, I am most heartily glad to see you: Sir, I solicit your connections. Hey Jack – what this is Mr Faulkland, who –

ABSOLUTE. Aye, Bob, Miss Melville's Mr Faulkland.

ACRES. Odso! she and your father can be but just arrived before me – I suppose you have seen them. Ah! Mr Faulkland, you are indeed a happy man.

FAULKLAND. I have not seen Miss Melville yet, Sir – I hope she enjoyed full health and spirits in Devonshire?

ACRES. Never knew her better in my life, Sir – never better. Odds blushes and blooms! she has been as healthy as the German Spa.

FAULKLAND. Indeed! – I did hear that she had been a little indisposed.

ACRES. False, false, Sir, only said to vex you: quite the reverse, I assure you.

FAULKLAND. There, Jack, you see she has the advantage of me; I had almost fretted myself ill.

ABSOLUTE. Now you are angry with your mistress for not having been sick.

FAULKLAND. No, no, you misunderstand me: yet surely a little trifling indisposition is not an unnatural consequence of absence from those we love. Now confess – isn't there something unkind in this violent, robust, unfeeling health?

ABSOLUTE. Oh, it was very unkind of her to be well in your absence to be sure!

ACRES. Good apartments, Jack.

FAULKLAND. Well Sir, but you were saying that Miss Melville has been so *exceedingly* well – what then she has been merry and gay I suppose? Always in spirits – hey?

ACRES. Merry, odds crickets! she has been the belle and spirit of the company wherever she has been – so lively and entertaining! so full of wit and humour!

FAULKLAND. There, Jack, there. Oh, by my soul! there is an innate levity in woman, that nothing can overcome. What! happy, and I away!

ABSOLUTE. Have done: how foolish this is! Just now you were only apprehensive for your mistress's spirits.

FAULKLAND. Why Jack, have I been the joy and spirit of the company?

ABSOLUTE. No indeed, you have not.

FAULKLAND. Have I been lively and entertaining?

ABSOLUTE. Oh, upon my word, I acquit you.

FAULKLAND. Have I been full of wit and humour?

ABSOLUTE. No, faith, to do you justice, you have been confoundedly stupid indeed.

ACRES. What's the matter with this gentleman?

ABSOLUTE. He is only expressing his great satisfaction at hearing that Julia has been so well and happy – that's all – hey, Faulkland?

FAULKLAND. Oh! I am rejoiced to hear it – yes, yes, she has a *happy* disposition!

ACRES. That she has indeed – then she is so accomplished so sweet a voice – so expert at her harpsichord – such a mistress of flat and sharp, squallante, rumblante, and quiverante! There was this time month – odds minims and crotchets! how she did chirrup at Mrs Piano's concert.

FAULKLAND. There again, what say you to this? You see she has been all mirth and song – not a thought of me!

ABSOLUTE. Pho! man, is not music the food of love?

FAULKLAND. Well, well, it may be so. Pray Mr – [*Aside to* ABSOLUTE.] – what's his damned name? – Do you remember what songs Miss Melville sung?

ACRES. Not I, indeed.

ABSOLUTE. Stay now, they were some pretty, melancholy, purling stream airs, I warrant; perhaps you may recollect: did she sing 'When absent from my soul's delight'?

ACRES. No, that wa'n't it.

ABSOLUTE. Or 'Go, gentle gales!' – (*Sings.*) 'Go, gentle gales!'

ACRES. O no! nothing like it. Odds! now I recollect one of them – (*Sings.*) 'My heart's my own, my will is free'.

FAULKLAND. Fool! fool that I am! to fix all my happiness on such a trifler! 'Sdeath! to make herself the pipe and balladmonger of a circle! to soothe her light heart with catches and glees! What can you say to this, Sir?

ABSOLUTE. Why, that I should be glad to hear my mistress had been so merry, Sir.

FAULKLAND. Nay, nay, nay – I am not sorry that she has been happy – no, no, I am glad of that – I would not have had her sad or sick – yet surely a sympathetic heart would have shown itself even in the choice of a song – she might have been temperately healthy, and somehow, plaintively gay; but she has been dancing too, I doubt not!

ACRES. What does the gentleman say about dancing?

ABSOLUTE. He says the lady we speak of dances as well as she sings.

ACRES. Aye truly, does she – there was at our last race-ball –

FAULKLAND. Hell and the devil! There! there! – I told you so! I told you so! Oh! she thrives in my absence! – dancing! – but her whole feelings have been in opposition with mine. I have been anxious, silent, pensive, sedentary – my days have been hours of care, my nights of watchfulness. She has been all health! spirit! laugh! song! dance! – Oh! damned, damned levity!

ABSOLUTE. For heaven's sake! Faulkland, don't expose yourself so. Suppose she has danced, what then? does not the ceremony of society often oblige –

FAULKLAND. Well, well, I'll contain myself – perhaps, as you say – for form sake. What, Mr Acres, you were praising Miss Melville's manner of dancing a minuet – hey?

ACRES. Oh, I dare insure her for that – but what I was going to speak of was her country dancing: odds swimmings! she has such an air with her!

FAULKLAND. Now disappointment on her! Defend this, Absolute, why don't you defend this? Country dances! jigs, and reels! am I to blame now? A minuet I could have forgiven – I should not have minded that – I say I should not have regarded a minuet – but *country dances!* Zounds! had she made one in a cotillon – I believe I could have forgiven even that – but to be monkey-led for a night! – to run the gauntlet through a string of amorous palming puppies! – to show paces like a managed filly! O Jack, there never can be but *one* man in the world, whom a truly modest and delicate woman ought to pair with in a country dance; and even then, the rest of the couples should be her great uncles and aunts!

ABSOLUTE. Aye, to be sure! grandfathers and grandmothers!

FAULKLAND. If there be but one vicious mind in the set, 'twill spread like a contagion – the action of their pulse beats to the lascivious movement of the jig – their quivering, warm-breathed sighs impregnate the very air – the atmosphere becomes electrical to love, and each amorous spark darts through every link of the chain! I must leave you – I own I am somewhat flurried – and that confounded looby has perceived it.

Going.

ABSOLUTE. Nay, but stay Faulkland, and thank Mr Acres for his good news.

FAULKLAND. Damn his news!

Exit FAULKLAND.

ABSOLUTE. Ha! ha! ha! poor Faulkland five minutes since – 'nothing on earth could give him a moment's uneasiness'!

ACRES. The gentleman wa'n't angry at my praising his mistress, was he?

ABSOLUTE. A little jealous, I believe, Bob.

ACRES. You don't say so? Ha! ha! jealous of me – that's a good joke.

ABSOLUTE. There's nothing strange in that, Bob: let me tell you, that sprightly grace and insinuating manner of yours will do some mischief among the girls here.

ACRES. Ah! you joke – ha! ha! mischief – ha! ha! but you know I am not my own property, my dear Lydia has forestalled me. She could never abide me in the country, because I used to dress so badly – but odds frogs and tambours! I shan't take matters so here – now ancient Madam has no voice in it – I'll make my old clothes know who's master – I shall straightway cashier the hunting-frock – and render my leather breeches incapable. My hair has been in training some time.

ABSOLUTE. Indeed!

ACRES. Aye and tho'ff the side-curls are a little restive, my hind-part takes to it very kindly.

ABSOLUTE. Oh, you'll polish, I doubt not.

ACRES. Absolutely I propose so – then if I can find out this Ensign Beverley, odds triggers and flints! I'll make him know the difference o't.

ABSOLUTE. Spoke like a man – but pray, Bob, I observe you have got an odd kind of a new method of swearing –

ACRES. Ha! ha! you've taken notice of it – 'tis genteel, isn't it? I didn't invent it myself though; but a commander in our militia – a great scholar, I assure you says that there is no meaning in the common oaths, and that nothing but their antiquity makes them respectable; because, he says, the ancients would never stick to an oath or two, but would say by Jove! or by Bacchus! or by Mars! or by Venus! or by Pallas! according to the sentiment – so that to swear with propriety, says my little major, the 'oath should be an echo to the sense', and this we call the *oath referential*, or *sentimental swearing* – ha! ha! ha! 'tis genteel, isn't it?

ABSOLUTE. Very genteel, and very new indeed – and I dare say will supplant all other figures of imprecation.

ACRES Aye, aye, the best terms will grow obsolete – damns have had their day.

Enter FAG.

FAG. Sir, there is a gentleman below, desires to see you – shall I show him into the parlour?

ABSOLUTE. Aye – you may.

ACRES. Well, I must be gone –

ABSOLUTE. Stay; who is it, Fag?

FAG. Your father, Sir.

ABSOLUTE. You puppy, why didn't you show him up directly?

Exit FAG.

ACRES. You have business with Sir Anthony – I expect a message from Mrs Malaprop at my lodgings – I have sent also to my dear friend Sir Lucius O'Trigger. Adieu, Jack, we must meet at night. Odds bottles and glasses! you shall give me a dozen bumpers to little Lydia.

ABSOLUTE. That I will with all my heart.

Exit ACRES.

ABSOLUTE. Now for a parental lecture – I hope he has heard nothing of the business that has brought me here. I wish the gout had held him fast in Devonshire, with all my soul!

Enter SIR ANTHONY.

Sir, I am delighted to see you here; and looking so well! – your sudden arrival at Bath made me apprehensive for your health.

SIR ANTHONY. Very apprehensive, I dare say, Jack. What, you are recruiting here, hey?

ABSOLUTE. Yes, Sir, I am on duty.

SIR ANTHONY. Well, Jack, I am glad to see you, though I did not expect it, for I was going to write to you on a little matter of business. Jack, I have been considering that I grow old and infirm, and shall probably not trouble you long.

ABSOLUTE. Pardon me, Sir, I never saw you look more strong and hearty; and I pray frequently that you may continue so.

SIR ANTHONY. I hope your prayers may be heard with all my heart. Well then, Jack, I have been considering that I am so strong and hearty, I may continue to plague you a long time. Now, Jack, I am sensible that the income of your commission, and what I have hitherto allowed you, is but a small pittance for a lad of your spirit.

ABSOLUTE. Sir, you are very good.

SIR ANTHONY. And it is my wish, while yet I live, to have my boy make some figure in the world. I have resolved, therefore, to fix you at once in a noble independence.

ABSOLUTE. Sir, your kindness overpowers me – such generosity makes the gratitude of reason more lively than the sensations even of filial affection.

SIR ANTHONY. I am glad you are so sensible of my attention – and you shall be master of a large estate in a few weeks.

ABSOLUTE. Let my future life, Sir, speak my gratitude: I cannot express the sense I have of your munificence. – Yet, Sir, I presume you would not wish me to quit the army?

SIR ANTHONY. Oh, that shall be as your wife chooses.

ABSOLUTE. My wife, Sir!

SIR ANTHONY. Aye, aye, settle that between you – settle that between you.

ABSOLUTE. A *wife*, Sir, did you say?

SIR ANTHONY. Aye, a wife – why, did not I mention her before?

ABSOLUTE. Not a word of her, Sir.

SIR ANTHONY. Odso! – I mustn't forget her though. Yes, Jack, the independence I was talking of is by a marriage – the fortune is saddled with a wife – but I suppose that makes no difference.

ABSOLUTE. Sir! Sir! – you amaze me!

SIR ANTHONY. Why, what the devil's the matter with the fool? Just now you were all gratitude and duty.

ABSOLUTE. I was, Sir – you talked to me of independence and a fortune, but not a word of a wife.

SIR ANTHONY. Why – what difference does that make? Odds life, Sir! if you have the estate, you must take it with the live stock on it, as it stands.

ABSOLUTE. If my happiness is to be the price, I must beg leave to decline the purchase. Pray, Sir, who is the lady?

SIR ANTHONY. What's that to you, Sir? Come, give me your promise to love, and to marry her directly.

ABSOLUTE. Sure, Sir, this is not very reasonable, to summon my affections for a lady I know nothing of!

SIR ANTHONY. I am sure, Sir, 'tis more unreasonable in you to *object* to a lady you know nothing of.

ABSOLUTE. Then, Sir, I must tell you plainly, that my inclinations are fixed on another – my heart is engaged to an angel.

SIR ANTHONY. Then pray let it send an excuse. It is very sorry – but *business* prevents its waiting on her.

ABSOLUTE. But my vows are pledged to her.

SIR ANTHONY. Let her foreclose, Jack; let her foreclose; they are not worth redeeming: besides, you have the angel's vows in exchange, I suppose; so there can be no loss there.

ABSOLUTE. You must excuse me, Sir, if I tell you, once for all, that in this point I cannot obey you.

SIR ANTHONY. Harkee Jack; I have heard you for some time with patience – I have been cool, quite cool; but take care – you know I am compliance itself – when I am not thwarted; no one more easily led – when I have my own way; but don't put me in a frenzy.

ABSOLUTE. Sir, I must repeat it – in this I cannot obey you.

SIR ANTHONY. Now, damn me! if ever I call you Jack again while I live!

ABSOLUTE. Nay, Sir, but hear me.

SIR ANTHONY. Sir, I won't hear a word – not a word! not one word! give me your promise by a nod and I'll tell you what Jack – I mean, you dog – if you don't, by –

ABSOLUTE. What, Sir, promise to link myself to some mass of ugliness! to –

SIR ANTHONY. Zounds! sirrah! the lady shall be as ugly as I choose: she shall have a hump on each shoulder; she shall be as crooked as the Crescent, her one eye shall roll like the bull's in Cox's museum – she shall have a skin like a mummy, and the beard of a Jew – she shall be all this, sirrah! – yet I'll make you ogle her all day, and sit up all night to write sonnets on her beauty.

ABSOLUTE. This is reason and moderation indeed!

SIR ANTHONY. None of your sneering, puppy! no grinning, jackanapes!

ABSOLUTE. Indeed, Sir, I never was in a worse humour for mirth in my life.

SIR ANTHONY. 'tis false, Sir! I know you are laughing in your sleeve: I know you'll grin when I am gone, sirrah!

ABSOLUTE. Sir, I hope I know my duty better.

SIR ANTHONY. None of your passion, Sir! none of your violence! if you please. It won't do with me, I promise you.

ABSOLUTE. Indeed, Sir, I never was cooler in my life.

SIR ANTHONY. 'tis a confounded lie! I know you are in a passion in your heart; I know you are, you hypocritical young dog! but it won't do.

ABSOLUTE. Nay, Sir, upon my word.

SIR ANTHONY. So you will fly out! Can't you be cool, like me? What the devil good can *passion* do! *Passion is* of no service, you impudent, insolent, overbearing reprobate! There you sneer again! don't provoke me! – but you rely upon the mildness of my temper – you do, you dog! you play upon the meekness of my disposition! Yet take care. – the patience of a saint may be overcome at last! – but mark! I give you six hours and a half to consider of this: if you then agree, without any condition, to do everything on earth that I choose, why confound you! I may in time forgive you – If not, zounds! don't enter the same hemisphere with me! don't dare to breathe the same air, or use the same light with me; but get an atmosphere and a sun of your own! I'll strip you of your commission – I'll lodge a five and threepence in the hands of trustees, and you shall live on the interest. I'll disown you, I'll disinherit you, I'll unget you! And damn me, if ever I call you Jack again!

Exit SIR ANTHONY ABSOLUTE.

ABSOLUTE. Mild, gentle, considerate father – I kiss your hands. What a tender method of giving his opinion in these matters Sir Anthony has! I dare not trust him with the truth. I wonder what old, wealthy hag it is that he wants to bestow on me! – yet he himself married for love, and was in his youth a bold intriguer, and a gay companion!

Enter FAG.

FAG. Assuredly, Sir, our father is wrath to a degree; he comes down stairs eight or ten steps at a time – muttering, growling, and thumping the banisters all the way: I, and the cook's dog, stand bowing at the door – rap! he gives me a stroke on the head with his cane – bids me carry that to my master, then kicking the poor turnspit into the area, damns us all, for a puppy triumvirate! – Upon my credit, Sir, were I in your place, and found my father such very bad company, I should certainly drop his acquaintance.

ABSOLUTE. Cease your impertinence, Sir, at present. Did you come in for nothing more? Stand out of the way!

Pushes him aside, and exit.

FAG. So! Sir Anthony trims my master; he is afraid to reply to his father – then vents his spleen on poor Fag! When one is vexed by one person, to revenge oneself on another, who happens to come in the way – is the vilest injustice! Ah! it shows the worst temper – the basest –

Enter ERRAND BOY

ERRAND BOY. Mr Fag! Mr Fag! your master calls you.

FAG. Well, you little, dirty puppy, you need not bawl so! – The meanest disposition! the –

ERRAND BOY. Quick, quick, Mr Fag.

FAG. *Quick, quick,* you impudent jackanapes! Am I to be commanded by you too? You little, impertinent, insolent kitchen-bred –

Exit, kicking and beating him.

Scene ii

The North Parade. Enter LUCY.

LUCY. So – I shall have another rival to add to my mistress's list – Captain Absolute. – However, I shall not enter his name till my purse has received notice in form. Poor Acres is dismissed! Well, I have done him a last friendly office, in letting him know that Beverley was here before him. Sir Lucius is generally more punctual when he expects to hear from his *dear Dalia,* as he calls her: I wonder he's not here! I have a little scruple of conscience from this deceit; though I should not be paid so well, if my hero knew that Delia was near fifty, and her own mistress.

Enter SIR LUCIUS O'TRIGGER.

SIR LUCIUS. Hah! my little embassadress – upon my conscience I have been looking for you; I have been on the South Parade this half-hour.

LUCY (*speaking simply*). O gemini! and I have been waiting for your
  worship here on the North.

SIR LUCIUS. Faith! – maybe that was the reason we did not meet;
  and it is very comical too, how you could go out and I not see you
  – for I was only taking a nap at the Parade coffeehouse, and I
  chose the window on purpose that I might not miss you.

LUCY. My stars! Now I'd wager a sixpence I went by while you
  were asleep.

SIR LUCIUS. Sure enough it must have been so and I never dreamt
  it was so late, till I waked. Well, but my little girl, have you got
  nothing for me?

LUCY. Yes, but I have – I've got a letter for you in my pocket.

SIR LUCIUS. O faith! I guessed you weren't come empty-handed –
  well – let me see what the dear creature says.

LUCY. There, Sir Lucius. *Gives him a letter*

SIR LUCIUS (*reads*). *Sir – there is often a sudden incentive impulse in love,
  that has a greater induction than years of domestic combination: such was the
  commotion I felt at the first superfluous view of Sir Lucius O'Trigger.* Very
  pretty, upon my word. *Female punctuation forbids me to say more, yet let
  me add, that it will give me joy infallible to find Sir Lucius worthy the last
  criterion of my affections. – Delia.* Upon my conscience! Lucy, your
  lady is a great mistress of language. Faith, she's quite the queen of
  the dictionary! – for the devil a word dare refuse coming at her
  call – though one would think it was quite out of hearing.

LUCY. Aye, Sir, a lady of her experience.

SIR LUCIUS. Experience! What, at seventeen?

LUCY. O true, Sir – but then she reads so – my stars! how she will
  read off-hand!

SIR LUCIUS. Faith, she must be very deep read to write this way –
  though she is a rather arbitrary writer too – for here are a great
  many poor words pressed into the service of this note, that would
  get their *habeas corpus* from any court in Christendom. – However,

when affection guides the pen, Lucy, he must be a brute who finds fault with the style.

LUCY. Ah! Sir Lucius, if you were to hear how she talks of you!

SIR LUCIUS. O tell her, I'll make her the best husband in the world, and Lady O' Trigger into the bargain! But we must get the old gentlewoman's consent – and do everything fairly.

LUCY. Nay, Sir Lucius, I thought you wa'n't rich enough to be so nice!

SIR LUCIUS. Upon my word, young woman, you have hit it: I am so poor that I can't afford to do a dirty action. If I did not want money I'd steal your mistress and her fortune with a great deal of pleasure. – However, my pretty girl, (*Gives her money.*) here's a little something to buy you a riband; and meet me in the evening, and I'll give you an answer to this. So, hussy, take a kiss beforehand, to put you in mind.

Kisses her.

LUCY. O Lud! Sir Lucius – I never seed such a gemman! My lady won't like you if you're so impudent.

SIR LUCIUS. Faith she will, Lucy – that same – pho! what's the name of it? – modesty! – is a quality in a lover more praised by the women than liked; so, if your mistress asks you whether Sir Lucius ever gave you a kiss, tell her *fifty* – my dear.

LUCY. What, would you have me tell her a lie?

SIR LUCIUS. Ah then, you baggage! I'll make it a truth presently.

LUCY. For shame now; here is someone coming.

SIR LUCIUS. O faith, I'll quiet your conscience!

Sees FAG. *Exit* [SIR LUCIUS], *humming a tune.*

Enter FAG.

FAG. So, so, Ma'am. I humbly beg pardon.

LUCY. O Lud! – now, Mr Fag, you flurry one so.

FAG. Come, come, Lucy, here's no one by so a little less simplicity, with a grain or two more sincerity, if you please. – You play false with us, Madam. I saw you give the Baronet a letter. My master shall know this – and if he doesn't call him out – I will.

LUCY. Ha! ha! ha! you gentlemen's gentlemen are so hasty. That letter was from Mrs Malaprop, simpleton. She is taken with Sir Lucius's address.

FAG. What tastes some people have! Why I suppose I have walked by her window an hundred times. – But what says our young lady? Any message to my master?

LUCY. Sad news! Mr Fag. A worse rival than Acres! Sir Anthony Absolute has proposed his son.

FAG. What, Captain Absolute?

LUCY. Even so – I overheard it all.

FAG. Ha! ha! ha! – very good, faith. Goodbye, Lucy, I must away with this news.

LUCY. Well – you may laugh – but it is true, I assure you. (*Going.*) But, Mr Fag, tell your master not to be cast down by this.

FAG. Oh, he'll be so disconsolate!

LUCY. And charge him not to think of quarrelling with young Absolute.

FAG. Never fear! – never fear!

LUCY. Be sure – bid him keep up his spirits.

FAG. We will – we will.

Exeunt severally.

Act III, Scene i

The North Parade. Enter ABSOLUTE.

ABSOLUTE. 'Tis just as Fag told me, indeed. Whimsical enough, faith! My father wants to force me to marry the very girl I am plotting to run away with! He must not know of my connection with her yet awhile. – He has too summary a method of proceeding in these matters and Lydia shall not yet lose her hopes of an elopement. – However, I'll read my recantation instantly. My conversion is something sudden, indeed, but I can assure him it is very *sincere*. – *So, so* – here he comes. He looks plaguy gruff.

Steps aside. Enter SIR ANTHONY.

SIR ANTHONY. No – I'll die sooner than forgive him. *Die*, did I say? I'll live these fifty years to plague him. – At our last meeting, his impudence had almost put me out of temper. An obstinate, passionate, self-willed boy! Who can he take after? This is my return for getting him before all his brothers and sisters! – for putting him, at twelve years old, into a marching regiment, and allowing him fifty pounds a year, besides his pay ever since! But I have done with him – he's anybody's son for me. – I never will see him more – never – never – never – never.

ABSOLUTE. Now for a penitential face. [*Advances.*]

SIR ANTHONY. Fellow, get out of my way.

ABSOLUTE. Sir, you see a penitent before you.

SIR ANTHONY. I see an impudent scoundrel before me.

ABSOLUTE. A sincere penitent. – I am come, Sir, to acknowledge my error, and to submit entirely to your will.

SIR ANTHONY. What's that?

ABSOLUTE. I have been revolving, and reflecting, and considering on your past goodness, and kindness, and condescension to me.

SIR ANTHONY. Well, Sir?

ABSOLUTE. I have likewise been weighing and balancing what you were pleased to mention concerning duty, and obedience, and authority.

SIR ANTHONY. Well, puppy?

ABSOLUTE. Why then, Sir, the result of my reflections is – a resolution to sacrifice every inclination of my own to your satisfaction.

SIR ANTHONY. Why now, you talk sense – absolute sense – I never heard anything more sensible in my life. – Confound you; you shall be *Jack* again.

ABSOLUTE. I am happy in the appellation.

SIR ANTHONY. Why, then, Jack, my dear Jack, I will now inform you who the lady really is. – Nothing but your passion and violence, you silly fellow, prevented my telling you at first. Prepare, Jack, for wonder and rapture – prepare. What think you of Miss Lydia Languish?

ABSOLUTE. Languish! What, the Languishes of Worcestershire?

SIR ANTHONY. Worcestershire! No. Did you never meet Mrs Malaprop and her niece, Miss Languish, who came into our country just before you were last ordered to your regiment?

ABSOLUTE. Malaprop! Languish! I don't remember ever to have heard the names before. Yet, stay – I think I do recollect something. – Languish! Languish! She squints, don't she? A little, red-haired girl?

SIR ANTHONY. Squints? A red-haired girl! Zounds, no.

ABSOLUTE. Then I must have forgot; it can't be the same person.

SIR ANTHONY. Jack! Jack! what think you of blooming, love-breathing seventeen?

ABSOLUTE. As to that, Sir, I am quite indifferent. If I can please you in the matter, 'tis all I desire.

SIR ANTHONY. Nay, but Jack, such eyes! such eyes! so innocently wild! so bashfully irresolute! Not a glance but speaks and kindles some thought of love! Then, Jack, her cheeks! her cheeks, Jack! so deeply blushing at the insinuations of her tell-tale eyes! Then, Jack, her lips! O Jack, lips smiling at their own discretion; and if not smiling, more sweetly pouting; more lovely in sullenness!

ABSOLUTE [*aside*]. That's she indeed. Well done, old gentleman!

SIR ANTHONY. Then, Jack, her neck. O Jack! Jack!

ABSOLUTE. And which is to be mine, Sir, the niece or the aunt?

SIR ANTHONY. Why, you unfeeling, insensible puppy, I despise you. When I was of your age, such a description would have made me fly like a rocket! The *aunt*, indeed! Odds life! when I ran away with your mother, I would not have touched anything old or ugly to gain an empire.

ABSOLUTE. Not to please your father, Sir?

SIR ANTHONY. To please my father! Zounds! not to please – O my father! – odso! – yes – yes! if my father indeed had desired – that's quite another matter. Though he wa'n't the indulgent father that I am, Jack.

ABSOLUTE. I dare say not, Sir.

SIR ANTHONY. But, Jack, you are not sorry to find your mistress is so beautiful.

ABSOLUTE. Sir, I repeat it; if I please you in this affair, 'tis all I desire. Not that I think a woman the worse for being handsome; but, Sir, if you please to recollect, you before hinted something about a hump or two, one eye, and a few more graces of that kind – now, without being very nice, I own I should rather choose a wife of mine to have the usual number of limbs, and a limited quantity of back: and though *one* eye may be very agreeable, yet as the prejudice has always run in favour of *two*, I would not wish to affect a singularity in that article.

SIR ANTHONY. What a phlegmatic sot it is! Why, sirrah, you're an anchorite! – a vile insensible stock. You a soldier! – you're a walking block, fit only to dust the company's regimentals on – odds life! I've a great mind to marry the girl myself.

ABSOLUTE. I am entirely at your disposal, Sir; if you should think of addressing Miss Languish yourself, I suppose you would have me marry the aunt; or if you should change your mind, and take the old lady – 'tis the same to me – I'll marry the niece.

SIR ANTHONY. Upon my word, Jack, thou'rt either a very great hypocrite or – but come, I know your indifference on such a subject must be all a lie – I'm sure it must – come, now – damn your demure face! – come, confess, Jack – you have been lying – ha'n't you? You have been playing the hypocrite, hey! – I'll never forgive you, if you ha'n't been lying and playing the hypocrite.

ABSOLUTE. I'm sorry, Sir, that the respect and duty which I bear to you should be so mistaken.

SIR ANTHONY. Hang your respect and duty! But, come along with me, I'll write a note to Mrs Malaprop, and you shall visit the lady directly.

ABSOLUTE. Where does she lodge, Sir?

SIR ANTHONY. What a dull question! – only on the Grove here.

ABSOLUTE. Oh! then I can call on her in my way to the coffee-house.

SIR ANTHONY. In your way to the coffee-house! You'll set your heart down in your way to the coffee-house, hey? Ah! you leaden-nerved, wooden-hearted dolt! But come along, you shall see her directly – her eyes shall be the Promethean torch to you – come along, I'll never forgive you, if you don't come back, stark mad with rapture and impatience – if you don't, egad, I'll marry the girl myself!

Exeunt.

Scene ii

JULIA'S *dressing-room.* FAULKLAND *solus.*

FAULKLAND. They told me Julia would return directly, I wonder she is not yet come! How mean does this captious, unsatisfied temper of mine appear to my cooler judgment! Yet I know not that I indulge it in any other point: but on this one subject, and to this one object, whom I think I love beyond my life, I am ever ungenerously fretful, and madly capricious! I am conscious of it – yet I cannot correct myself! What tender, honest joy sparkled in her eyes when we met! How delicate was the warmth of her expressions! I was ashamed to appear less happy – though I had come resolved to wear a face of coolness and upbraiding. Sir Anthony's presence prevented my proposed expostulations: yet I must be satisfied that she has not been so very happy in my absence. – She is coming! – yes! – I know the nimbleness of her tread, when she thinks her impatient Faulkland counts the moments of her stay.

Enter JULIA.

JULIA. I had not hoped to see you again so soon.

FAULKLAND. Could I, Julia, be contented with my first welcome – restrained as we were by the presence of a third person?

JULIA O Faulkland, when your kindness can make me thus happy, let me not think that I discovered something of coldness in your first salutation.

FAULKLAND. 'Twas but your fancy, Julia. I *was* rejoiced to see you – to see you in such health – sure I had no cause for coldness?

JULIA. Nay then, I see you have taken something ill. You must not conceal from me what it is.

FAULKLAND. Well then – shall I own to you that my joy at hearing of your health and arrival here, by your neighbour Acres, was somewhat damped, by his dwelling much on the high spirits you had enjoyed in Devonshire – on your mirth – your singing – dancing, and I know not what! For such is my temper, Julia, that

I should regard every mirthful moment in your absence as a treason to constancy: the mutual tear that steals down the cheek of parting lovers is a compact, that no smile shall live there till they meet again.

JULIA. Must I never cease to tax my Faulkland with this teasing minute caprice? Can the idle reports of a silly boor weigh in your breast against my tried affection?

FAULKLAND. They have no weight with me, Julia: no, no – I am happy if you have been so – yet only say, that you did not sing with *mirth* – say that you *thought* of Faulkland in the dance.

JULIA. I never can be happy in your absence. If I wear a countenance of content, it is to show that my mind holds no doubt of my Faulkland's truth. If I seemed sad, it were to make malice triumph; and say, that I had fixed my heart on one, who left me to lament his roving, and my own credulity. Believe me, Faulkland, I mean not to upbraid you, when I say, that I have often dressed sorrow in smiles, lest my friends should guess whose unkindness had caused my tears.

FAULKLAND. You were ever all goodness to me. Oh, I am a brute, when I but admit a doubt of your true constancy!

JULIA. If ever, without such cause from you as I will not suppose possible, you find my affections veering but a point, may I become a proverbial scoff for levity, and base ingratitude.

FAULKLAND. Ah! Julia, that *last* word is grating to me. I would I had no title to your *gratitude*! Search your heart, Julia; perhaps what you have mistaken for love is but the warm effusion of a too thankful heart!

JULIA. For what quality must I love you?

FAULKLAND. For no quality! To regard me for any quality of mind or understanding, were only to *esteem* me. And for person – I have often wished myself deformed, to be convinced that I owed no obligation there for any part of your affection.

JULIA. Where nature has bestowed a show of nice attention in the features of a man, he should laugh at it, as misplaced. I have seen men, who in *this* vain article perhaps might rank above you; but my heart has never asked my eyes whether it were so or not.

FAULKLAND. Now this is not well from *you*, Julia – I despise person in a man. Yet if you loved me as I wish, though I were an Ethiop, you'd think none so fair.

JULIA. I see you are determined to be unkind. The contract which my poor father bound us in gives you more than a lover's privilege.

FAULKLAND. Again, Julia, you raise ideas that feed and justify my doubts. I would not have been more free – no – I am proud of my restraint – yet – yet – perhaps your high respect alone for this solemn compact has fettered your inclinations, which else had made a worthier choice. How shall I be sure, had you remained unbound in thought and promise, that I should still have been the object of your persevering love?

JULIA. Then try me now. Let us be free as strangers as to what is past: *my* heart will not feel more liberty!

FAULKLAND. There now! so hasty, Julia! so anxious to be free! If your love for me were fixed and ardent, you would not loose your hold, even though I wished it!

JULIA. Oh, you torture me to the heart! I cannot bear it.

FAULKLAND. I do not mean to distress you. If I loved you less, I should never give you an uneasy moment. But hear me. All my fretful doubts arise from this – women are not used to weigh, and separate the motives of their affections: the cold dictates of prudence, gratitude, or filial duty, may sometimes be mistaken for the pleadings of the heart. – I would not boast – yet let me say, that I have neither age, person, or character, to found dislike on; my fortune such as few ladies could be charged with indiscretion in the match. O Julia! when *love* receives such countenance from *prudence*, nice minds will be suspicious of its birth.

JULIA. I know not whither your insinuations would tend: but as they seem pressing to insult me – I will spare you the regret of having done so. – I have given you no cause for this!

Exit in tears.

FAULKLAND. In tears! stay Julia, stay but for a moment. – The
door is fastened! – Julia! – my soul – but for one moment – I
hear her sobbing! 'Sdeath! what a brute am I to use her thus!
Yet stay – aye she is coming now: how little resolution there is in
woman! – how a few soft words can turn them! No, faith! she is
not coming either. Why, Julia – my love – say but that you forgive
me – come but to tell me that – now, this is being *too* resentful:
stay! she *is* coming too – I thought she would – no steadiness in
anything! Her going away must have been a mere trick then – she
shan't see that I was hurt by it. I'll affect indifference – (*Hums a
tune: then listens.*) – no – zounds! she's *not* coming!-nor don't intend
it, I suppose. This is not steadiness, but obstinacy! Yet I deserve it.
What, after so long an absence, to quarrel with her tenderness! –
'twas barbarous and unmanly! I should be ashamed to see her
now. I'll wait till her just resentment is abated – and when I
distress her so again, may I lose her for ever! and be linked
instead to some antique virago, whose gnawing passions, and
longhoarded spleen, shall make me curse my folly half the day,
and all the night!

Exit.

Scene iii

MRS MALAPROP*'s lodgings.* MRS MALAPROP, *and* CAPTAIN
ABSOLUTE.

MRS MALAPROP. Your being Sir Anthony's son, Captain, would
itself be a sufficient accommodation; but from the ingenuity of
your appearance, I am convinced you deserve the character here
given of you.

ABSOLUTE. Permit me to say, Madam, that as I never yet have
had the pleasure of seeing Miss Languish, my principal

inducement in this affair at present, is the honour of being allied to Mrs Malaprop; of whose intellectual accomplishments, e!elegant manners, and unaffected learning, no tongue is silent.

MRS MALAPROP. Sir, you do me infinite honour! I beg, Captain, you'll be seated. (*Sit.*) Ah! few gentlemen, nowadays, know how to value the ineffectual qualities in a woman! Few think how a little knowledge becomes a gentlewoman! Men have no sense now but for the worthless flower of beauty!

ABSOLUTE. It is but too true indeed, Ma'am – yet I fear our ladies should share the blame – they think our admiration of beauty so great, that knowledge in them would be superfluous. Thus, like garden-trees, they seldom show fruit, till time has robbed them of the more specious blossom. Few, like Mrs Malaprop and the orange-tree, are rich in both at once!

MRS MALAPROP. Sir – you overpower me with good-breeding. He is the very pineapple of politeness! You are not ignorant, Captain, that this giddy girl has somehow contrived to fix her affections on a beggarly, strolling, eavesdropping Ensign, whom none of us have seen, and nobody knows anything of.

ABSOLUTE. Oh, I have heard the silly affair before. I'm not at all prejudiced against her on that account.

MRS MALAPROP. You are very good, and very considerate, Captain. I am sure I have done everything in my power since I exploded the affair! Long ago I laid my positive conjunctions on her never to think on the fellow again – I have since laid Sir Anthony's preposition before her – but I'm sorry to say she seems resolved to decline every particle that I enjoin her.

ABSOLUTE. It must be very distressing indeed, Ma'am.

MRS MALAPROP. Oh! it gives me the hydrostatics to such a degree! I thought she had persisted from corresponding with him, but behold this very day, I have interceded another letter from the fellow! I believe I have it in my pocket.

ABSOLUTE (*aside*). O the devil! my last note.

MRS MALAPROP. Aye, here it is.

ABSOLUTE (*aside*). Aye, my note indeed! O the little traitress Lucy.

MRS MALAPROP. There, perhaps you may know the writing.

Gives him the letter.

ABSOLUTE. I think I have seen the hand before – yes, I certainly must have seen this hand before

MRS MALAPROP. Nay, but read it, Captain.

ABSOLUTE (*reads*). *'My soul's idol, my adored Lydia!'* Very tender indeed!

MRS MALAPROP. Tender! aye, and profane too, o' my conscience!

ABSOLUTE. *'I am excessively alarmed at the intelligence you send me, the more so as my new rival '* –

MRS MALAPROP. That's you, Sir.

ABSOLUTE. *'has universally the character of being an accomplished gentleman, and a man of honour.'* Well, that's handsome enough.

MRS MALAPROP. Oh, the fellow had some design in writing so –

ABSOLUTE. That he had, I'll answer for him, Ma'am.

MRS MALAPROP. But go on, Sir – you'll see presently.

ABSOLUTE. *'As for the old weather-beaten she-dragon who guards you'* – who can he mean by that?

MRS MALAPROP. *Me*, Sir – *me* – he means *me* there – what do you think now? But go on a little further.

ABSOLUTE. Impudent scoundrel! – *'it shall go hard but I will elude her vigilance, as l am told that the same ridiculous vanity, which makes her dress up her coarse features, and deck her dull chat with hard words which she don't understand'* –

MRS MALAPROP. There, Sir! an attack upon my language! What do you think of that? An aspersion upon my parts of speech! Was ever such a brute! Sure if I reprehend anything in this world, it is the use of my oracular tongue, and a nice derangement of epitaphs!

ABSOLUTE. He deserves to be hanged and quartered! Let me see – *'same ridiculous vanity'* –

MRS MALAPROP. You need not read it again, Sir.

ABSOLUTE. I beg pardon, Ma'am – *'does also lay her open to the grossest deceptions from flattery and pretended admiration'* – an impudent coxcomb! *'so that I have a scheme to see you shortly with the old harridan's consent, and even to make her a go-between in our interviews.'* – Was ever such assurance?

MRS MALAPROP. Did you ever hear anything like it? He'll elude my vigilance, will he? Yes, yes! ha! ha! He's very likely to enter these doors! – we'll try who can plot best.

ABSOLUTE. So we will Ma'am – so we will. Ha! ha! ha! A conceited puppy, ha! ha! ha! Well, but Mrs Malaprop, as the girl seems so infatuated by this fellow, suppose you were to wink at her corresponding with him for a little time – let her even plot an elopement with him – then do you connive at her escape – while I, just in the nick, will have the fellow laid by the heels, and fairly contrive to carry her off in his stead.

MRS MALAPROP. I am delighted with the scheme, never was anything better perpetrated!

ABSOLUTE. But, pray, could not I see the lady for a few minutes now? I should like to try her temper a little.

MRS MALAPROP. Why, I don't know – I doubt she is not prepared for a visit of this kind. There is a decorum in these matters.

ABSOLUTE. O Lord! she won't mind *me* – only tell her Beverley –

MRS MALAPROP. Sir!

ABSOLUTE (*aside*). Gently, good tongue.

MRS MALAPROP. What did you say of Beverley?

ABSOLUTE. Oh, I was going to propose that you should tell her, by way of jest, that it was Beverley who was below; she'd come down fast enough then – ha! ha! ha!

MRS MALAPROP. 'Twould be a trick she well deserves – besides you know the fellow tells her he'll get my consent to see her – ha! ha! Let him if he can, I say again. (*Calling.*) Lydia, come down here! He'll make me a *go-between in their interviews*! – ha! ha! ha! Come down, I say, Lydia! I don't wonder at your laughing, ha! ha! ha! His impudence is truly ridiculous.

ABSOLUTE. 'Tis very ridiculous, upon my soul, Ma'am, ha! ha! ha!

MRS MALAPROP. The little hussy won't hear. Well, I'll go and tell her at once who it is – she shall know that Captain Absolute is come to wait on her. And I'll make her behave as becomes a young woman.

ABSOLUTE. As you please, Ma'am.

MRS MALAPROP. For the present, Captain, your servant – oh! you've not done laughing yet, I see – *elude my vigilance!* Yes, yes, ha! ha! ha!

Exit.

ABSOLUTE. Ha! ha! ha! one would think now that I might throw off all disguise at once, and seize my prize with security – but such is Lydia's caprice, that to undeceive her were probably to lose her. I'll see whether she knows me.

Walks aside, and seems engaged in looking at the pictures. Enter LYDIA.

LYDIA. What a scene am I now to go through! Surely nothing can be more dreadful than to be obliged to listen to the loathsome addresses of a stranger to one's heart. I have heard of girls persecuted as I am, who have appealed in behalf of their favoured lover to the generosity of his rival: suppose I were to try it – there stands the hated rival – an officer too! – but oh, how unlike my Beverley! – I wonder he don't begin – truly he seems a very negligent wooer! Quite at his ease, upon my word! I'll speak first – Mr Absolute.

ABSOLUTE. Madam.

Turns round.

LYDIA. O heavens! Beverley!

ABSOLUTE. Hush! – hush, my life! – softly! be not surprised!

LYDIA. I am so astonished! and so terrified! and so overjoyed! For heaven's sake! how came you here?

ABSOLUTE. Briefly – I have deceived your aunt – I was informed that my new rival was to visit here this evening, and contriving to have him kept away, have passed myself on her for Captain Absolute.

LYDIA. O charming! And she really takes you for young Absolute?

ABSOLUTE. Oh, she's convinced of it.

LYDIA. Ha! ha! ha! I can't forbear laughing to think how her sagacity is overreached!

ABSOLUTE. But we trifle with our precious moments – such another opportunity may not occur – then let me now conjure my kind, my condescending angel, to fix the time when I may rescue her from undeserved persecution, and with a licensed warmth plead for my reward.

LYDIA. Will you then, Beverley, consent to forfeit that portion of my paltry wealth – that burden on the wings of love?

ABSOLUTE. Oh, come to me – rich only thus – in loveliness – bring no portion to me but thy love – 'twill be generous in you Lydia – for well you know, it is the only dower your poor Beverley can repay.

LYDIA. How persuasive are his words! How charming will poverty be with him!

ABSOLUTE. Ah! my soul, what a life will we then live? Love shall be our idol and support! We will worship him with a monastic strictness; abjuring all worldly toys, to centre every thought and action there. Proud of calamity, we will enjoy the wreck of wealth;

while the surrounding gloom of adversity shall make the flame of our pure love show doubly bright. – By heavens! I would fling all goods of fortune from me with a prodigal hand to enjoy the scene where I might clasp my Lydia to my bosom, and say, the world affords no smile to me – but here – (*Embracing her. Aside.*) If she holds out now the devil is in it!

LYDIA. Now could I fly with him to the Antipodes! but my persecution is not yet come to a crisis.

Enter MRS MALAPROP, *listening.*

MRS MALAPROP. I'm impatient to know how the little hussy deports herself.

ABSOLUTE. So pensive, Lydia! – is then your warmth abated?

MRS MALAPROP. *Warmth abated!* – so! she has been in a passion, I suppose.

LYDIA. No – nor ever can while I have life.

MRS MALAPROP. An ill-tempered little devil! She'll be in a passion all her life, will she?

LYDIA. Think not the idle threats of my ridiculous aunt can ever have any weight with me.

MRS MALAPROP. Very dutiful, upon my word!

LYDIA. Let her choice be Captain Absolute, but Beverley is mine.

MRS MALAPROP. I am astonished at her assurance! – to his face! – this to his face!

ABSOLUTE (*kneeling*). Thus then let me enforce my suit.

MRS MALAPROP. Aye – poor young man! – down on his knees entreating for pity! – I can contain no longer. – [*Reveals herself.*] Why thou vixen! – I have overheard you.

ABSOLUTE (*aside*). Oh, confound her vigilance!

MRS MALAPROP. Captain Absolute – I know not how to apologise for her shocking rudeness.

ABSOLUTE (*aside*). So – all's safe, I find. – I have hopes, Madam, that time will bring the young lady –

MRS MALAPROP. Oh there's nothing to be hoped for from her! She's as headstrong as an allegory on the banks of Nile.

LYDIA. Nay, Madam, what do you charge me with now?

MRS MALAPROP. Why, thou unblushing rebel – didn't you tell this gentleman to his face that you loved another better? Didn't you say you never would be his?

LYDIA. No, Madam – I did not.

MRS MALAPROP. Good heavens! what assurance! Lydia, Lydia, you ought to know that lying don't become a young woman! Didn't you boast that Beverley – that stroller Beverley, possessed your heart? Tell me that, I say.

LYDIA. 'Tis true, Ma'am, and none but Beverley

MRS MALAPROP. Hold; hold, Assurance! you shall not be so rude.

ABSOLUTE. Nay, pray Mrs Malaprop, don't stop the young lady's speech: she's very welcome to talk thus – it does not hurt *me* in the least, I assure you.

MRS MALAPROP. You are too good, Captain – *too* amiably patient – but come with me, Miss – let us see you again soon, Captain – remember what we have fixed.

ABSOLUTE. I shall, Ma'am.

MRS MALAPROP. Come, take a graceful leave of the gentleman.

LYDIA. May every blessing wait on my Beverley, my loved Bev –

MRS MALAPROP. Hussy! I'll choke the word in your throat! Come along – come along.

Exeunt severally, [ABSOLUTE] *kissing his hand to* LYDIA, MRS MALAPROP *stopping her from speaking.*

Scene iv

ACRES'S *lodgings.* ACRES *as just dressed and* DAVID.

ACRES. Indeed, David do you think I become it so?

DAVID. You are quite another creature, believe me Master, by the
mass! An' we've any luck we shall see the Devon monkeyrony in
all the print-shops in Bath!

ACRES. Dress *does* make a difference, David.

DAVID. 'Tis all in all, I think difference! Why, an' you were to go
now to Clod Hall, I am certain the old lady wouldn't know you:
Master Butler wouldn't believe his own eyes, and Mrs Pickle
would cry, 'Lard presarve me!'. Our dairymaid would come
giggling to the door, and I warrant Dolly Tester, your honour's
favourite, would blush like my waistcoat. Oons! I'll hold a gallon,
there an't a dog in the house but would bark, and I question
whether Phillis would wag a hair of her tail!

ACRES. Aye, David, there's nothing like *polishing*.

DAVID. So I says of your honour's boots; but the boy never heeds
me!

ACRES. But, David, has Mr De-la-Grace been here? I must rub up
my balancing, and chasing, and boring.

DAVID. I'll call again, Sir.

ACRES. Do – and see if there are any letters for me at the post
office.

DAVID. I will. – By the mass, I can't help looking at your head! If I
hadn't been by at the cooking, I wish I may die if I should have
known the dish again myself!

Exit. ACRES *comes forward, practising a dancing step.*

ACRES. Sink, slide – coupee – confound the first inventors of
cotillons! say I – they are as bad as algebra to us country
gentlemen – I can walk a minuet easy enough when I'm forced! –
and I have been accounted a good stick in a country dance.

Odds jigs and tabors! I never valued your cross over to couple –
figure in – right and left – and I'd foot it with e'er a captain in the
county! – but these outlandish heathen allemandes and cotillons
are quite beyond me! – I shall never prosper at 'em, that's sure –
mine are true-born English legs – they don't understand their
cursed French lingo! – their pas this, and pas that, and pas
t'other! damn me, my feet don't like to be called paws! No, 'tis
certain I have most antigallican toes!

Enter SERVANT.

SERVANT. Here is Sir Lucius O'Trigger to wait on you, Sir.

ACRES. Show him in.

Enter SIR LUCIUS.

SIR LUCIUS. Mr Acres, I am delighted to embrace you.

ACRES. My dear Sir Lucius, I kiss your hands.

SIR LUCIUS. Pray, my friend, what has brought you so suddenly to
Bath?

ACRES. Faith! I have followed Cupid's jack-o'-lantern, and find
myself in a quagmire at last. In short, I have been very ill-used,
Sir Lucius. I don't choose to mention names, but look on me as a
very ill-used gentleman.

SIR LUCIUS. Pray, what is the case? I ask no names.

ACRES. Mark me, Sir Lucius, I fall as deep as need be in love with a
young lady – her friends take my part – I follow her to Bath –
send word of my arrival, and receive answer, that the lady is to be
otherwise disposed of. This, Sir Lucius, I call being ill-used.

SIR LUCIUS. Very ill, upon my conscience. Pray, can you divine
the cause of it?

ACRES. Why, there's the matter: she has another lover, one
Beverley, who, I am told, is now in Bath. Odds slanders and lies!
he must be at the bottom of it.

SIR LUCIUS. A rival in the case, is there? And you think he has supplanted you unfairly?

ACRES. *Unfairly!* – to be sure he has. He never could have done it fairly.

SIR LUCIUS. Then sure you know what is to be done!

ACRES. Not I, upon my soul!

SIR LUCIUS. We wear no swords here, but you understand me.

ACRES. What! fight him!

SIR LUCIUS. Aye, to be sure: what can I mean else?

ACRES. But he has given me no provocation.

SIR LUCIUS. Now, I think he has given you the greatest provocation in the world. – Can a man commit a more heinous offence against another than to fall in love with the same woman? Oh, by my soul, it is the most unpardonable breach of friendship!

ACRES. Breach of *friendship*! Aye, aye; but I have no acquaintance with this man. I never saw him in my life.

SIR LUCIUS. That's no argument at all – he has the less right then to take such a liberty.

ACRES. Gad that's true – I grow full of anger, Sir Lucius! – I fire apace! Odds hilts and blades! I find a man may have a deal of valour in him, and not know it! But couldn't I contrive to have a little right of my side?

SIR LUCIUS. What the devil signifies *right*, when your *honour* is concerned? Do you think Achilles, or my little Alexander the Great ever inquired where the right lay? No, by my soul, they drew their broadswords, and left the lazy sons of peace to settle the justice of it.

ACRE S Your words are a grenadier's march to my heart! I believe courage must be catching! I certainly do feel a kind of valour rising as it were – a kind of courage, as I may say – odds flints, pans, and triggers! I'll challenge him directly.

SIR LUCIUS. Ah, my little friend! if we had Blunderbuss Hall here
– I could show you a range of ancestry, in the O'Trigger line, that
would furnish the new room, every one of whom had killed his
man! – For though the mansion-house and dirty acres have
slipped through my fingers, I thank heaven our honour, and the
family pictures, are as fresh as ever.

ACRES. O Sir Lucius! I have had ancestors too! Every man of 'em
colonel or captain in the militia! Odds balls and barrels! say no
more – I'm braced for it. The thunder of your words has soured
the milk of human kindness in my breast! Zounds! as the man in
the play says, 'I could do such deeds!'

SIR LUCIUS. Come, come, there must be no passion at all in the
case – these things should always be done civilly.

ACRES. I must be in a passion, Sir Lucius – I must be in a rage –
dear Sir Lucius, let me be in a rage, if you love me. – Come,
here's pen and paper. (*Sits down to write.*) I would the ink were red!
Indite, I say, indite! How shall I begin? Odds bullets and blades!
I'll write a good bold hand, however.

SIR LUCIUS. Pray compose yourself.

ACRES. Come – now shall I begin with an oath? Do, Sir Lucius, let
me begin with a damme.

SIR LUCIUS. Pho! pho! do the thing *decently* and like a Christian.
Begin now – [*Dictating to* ACRES.] '*Sir*' –

ACRES. That's too civil by half.

SIR LUCIUS. '*To prevent the confusion that might arise*' –

ACRES. Well –

SIR LUCIUS. '*From our both addressing the same lady*' –

ACRES. Aye – there's the reason – [*Writing.*] '*same lady*' – well –

SIR LUCIUS. '*I shall expect the honour of your company*' –

ACRES. Zounds! I'm not asking him to dinner.

SIR LUCIUS. Pray be easy.

ACRES. Well then, '*honour of your company*'.

SIR LUCIUS. '*To settle our pretensions*' –

ACRES. Well.

SIR LUCIUS. Let me see, aye, Kingsmead Fields will do. '*In Kingsmead Fields*'.

ACRES. So that's done. Well, I'll fold it up presently – my own crest – a hand and dagger shall be the seal.

SIR LUCIUS. You see now this little explanation will put a stop at once to all confusion or misunderstanding that might arise between you.

ACRES. Aye, we fight to prevent any misunderstanding.

SIR LUCIUS. Now, I'll leave you to fix your own time. Take my advice and you'll decide it this evening if you can – then let the worst come of it, 'twill be off your mind tomorrow.

ACRES. Very true.

SIR LUCIUS. So I shall see nothing more of you unless it be by letter till the evening. I would do myself the honour to carry your message; but, to tell you a secret, I believe I shall have just such another affair on my own hands. There is a gay captain here, who put a jest on me lately, at the expense of my country, and I only want to fall in with the gentleman, to call him out.

ACRES. By my valour, I should like to see you fight first! Odds life! I should like to see you kill him, if it was only to get a little lesson.

SIR LUCIUS. I shall be very proud of instructing you. – Well for the present – but remember now, when you meet your antagonist, do everything in a mild and agreeable manner. Let your courage be as keen, but at the same time as polished as your sword.

Exeunt severally

Act IV, Scene i

ACRES's *lodgings*. ACRES *and* DAVID.

DAVID. Then, by the mass, Sir! I would do no such thing – ne'er a Sir Lucius O'Trigger in the kingdom should make me fight, when I wa'n't so minded. Oons! what will the old lady say, when she hears o't!

ACRES. Ah! David, if you had heard Sir Lucius! – odds sparks and flames! he would have roused your valour.

DAVID. Not he, indeed. I hates such bloodthirsty cormorants. Lookee, Master, if you'd wanted a bout at boxing, quarterstaff, or short-staff, I should never be the man to bid you cry off: but for your cursed sharps and snaps, I never knew any good come of 'em.

ACRES. But my *honour*, David, my *honour*! *I* must be very careful of my honour.

DAVID. Aye, by the mass! and I would be very careful of it; and I think in return my honour couldn't do less than to be very careful of *me*.

ACRES. Odds blades! David, no gentleman will ever risk the loss of his honour!

DAVID. I say then, it would be but civil in honour never to risk the loss of the gentleman. – Lookee, Master, this honour seems to me to be a marvellous false friend; aye, truly, a very courtier-like servant. – Put the case, I was a gentleman (which, thank God, no one can say of me); well – my honour makes me quarrel with another gentleman of my acquaintance. So we fight (pleasant enough that). Boh! – I kill him (the more's my luck). Now, pray who gets the profit of it? Why, my honour. But put the case that he kills me! – by the mass! I go to the worms, and my honour whips over to my enemy!

ACRES. No, David – in that case – odds crowns and laurels! your honour follows you to the grave.

DAVID. Now, that's just the place where I could make a shift to do without it.

ACRES. Zounds, David! you're a coward! It doesn't become my valour to listen to you. What, shall I disgrace my ancestors? Think of that, David – think what it would be to disgrace my ancestors!

DAVID. Under favour, the surest way of not disgracing them, is to keep as long as you can out of their company. Lookee now, Master, to go to them in such haste – with an ounce of lead in your brains – I should think might as well be let alone. Our ancestors are very good kind of folks; but they are the last people I should choose to have a visiting acquaintance with.

ACRES. But David, now, you don't think there is such very, very, *very* great danger, hey? Odds life! people often fight without any mischief done!

DAVID. By the mass, I think 'tis ten to one against you! Oons! here to meet some lion-headed fellow, I warrant, with his damned double-barrelled swords, and cut and thrust pistols! Lord bless us! it makes me tremble to think o't! – Those be such desperate bloody-minded weapons! Well, I never could abide 'em – from a child I never could fancy 'em! I suppose there a'n't so merciless a beast in the world as your loaded pistol!

ACRES. Zounds! I *won't* be afraid – odds fire and fury! you shan't make me afraid. Here is the challenge, and I have sent for my dear friend Jack Absolute to carry it for me.

DAVID. Aye, i'the name of mischief, let *him* be the messenger. For my part, I wouldn't lend a hand to it for the best horse in your stable. By the mass! it don't look like another letter! It is, as I may say, a designing and malicious-looking letter! And I warrant smells of gunpowder like a soldier's pouch! Oons! I wouldn't swear it mayn't go off!

ACRES. Out, you poltroon! – You ha'n't the valour of a grasshopper.

DAVID. Well, I say no more – 'twill be sad news, to be sure, at Clod Hall! – but I ha' done. (*Whimpering*.) How Phillis will howl when she hears of it! aye, poor bitch, she little thinks what shooting her master's going after! And I warrant old Crop, who has carried your honour, field and road, these ten years, will curse the hour he was born.

ACRES. It won't do, David – I am determined to fight – so get along, you coward, while I'm in the mind.

Enter SERVANT.

SERVANT Captain Absolute, Sir.

ACRES. Oh! Show him up.

Exit SERVANT.

DAVID. Well, heaven send we be all alive this time tomorrow.

ACRES. What's that! Don't provoke me, David!

DAVID (*whimpering*). Goodbye, Master.

ACRES. Get along, you cowardly, dastardly, croaking raven.

Exit DAVID. *Enter* ABSOLUTE.

ABSOLUTE. What's the matter, Bob?

ACRES. A vile, sheep-hearted blockhead! If I hadn't the valour of St George and the dragon to boot –

ABSOLUTE. But what did you want with me, Bob?

ACRES. Oh! – there –

Gives him the challenge.

ABSOLUTE (*aside*). 'To Ensign Beverley.' So – what's going on now? – Well, what's this?

ACRES. A challenge!

ABSOLUTE. Indeed! Why, you won't fight him; will you, Bob?

ACRES. Egad but I will, Jack. Sir Lucius has wrought me to it. He has left me full of rage – and I'll fight this evening, that so much good passion mayn't be wasted.

ABSOLUTE. But what have I to do with this?

ACRES. Why, as I think you know something of this fellow, I want you to find him out for me, and give him this mortal *defiance*.

ABSOLUTE. Well, give it to me, and trust me he gets it.

ACRES. Thank you, my dear friend, my dear Jack; but it is giving you a great deal of trouble.

ABSOLUTE. Not in the least – I beg you won't mention it. No trouble in the world, I assure you.

ACRES. You are very kind. What it is to have a friend! You couldn't be my second – could you, Jack?

ABSOLUTE. Why no, Bob – not in *this* affair – it would not be quite so proper.

ACRES. Well then, I must get my friend Sir Lucius. I shall have your good wishes, however, Jack.

ABSOLUTE. Whenever he meets you, believe me.

Enter SERVANT.

SERVANT. Sir Anthony Absolute is below, inquiring for the Captain.

ABSOLUTE. I'll come instantly. – Well, my little hero, success attend you.

Going.

ACRES. Stay – stay, Jack. If Beverley should ask you what kind of a man your friend Acres is, do tell him I am a devil of a fellow – will you, Jack?

ABSOLUTE. To be sure I shall. I'll say you are a determined dog – hey, Bob!

ACRES. Aye, do, do – and if that frightens him, egad perhaps he mayn't come. So tell him I generally kill a man a week; will you, Jack?

ABSOLUTE. I will, I will; I'll say you are called in the country 'Fighting Bob'!

ACRES. Right, right – 'tis all to prevent mischief; for I don't want to take his life if I clear my honour.

ABSOLUTE. No! – that's very kind of you.

ACRES. Why, you don't wish me to kill him – do you, Jack?

ABSOLUTE. No, upon my soul, I do not. But a devil of a fellow, hey?

Going.

ACRES. True, true – but stay – stay, Jack – you may add that you never saw me in such a rage before – a most devouring rage!

ABSOLUTE. I will, I will.

ACRES. Remember, Jack – a determined dog!

ABSOLUTE. Aye, aye, 'Fighting Bob'!

Exeunt severally.

Scene ii

MRS MALAPROP's *lodgings*. MRS MALAPROP *and* LYDIA.

MRS MALAPROP. Why, thou perverse one! – tell me what you can object to him? Isn't he a handsome man? Tell me that. A genteel man? A pretty figure of a man?

LYDIA (*aside*). She little thinks whom she is praising! – So is Beverley, Ma'am.

MRS MALAPROP. No caparisons, Miss, if you please! Caparisons don't become a young woman. No! Captain Absolute is indeed a fine gentleman!

LYDIA (*aside*). Aye, the Captain Absolute *you* have seen.

MRS MALAPROP. Then he's *so* well bred – *so* full of alacrity, and adulation! – and has *so much* to say for himself: in such good language too! His physiognomy so grammatical! Then his presence is so noble! I protest, when I saw him, I thought of what Hamlet says in the play: 'Hesperian curls! – the front of Job himself! – an eye, like March, to threaten at command! – a station, like Harry Mercury, new' – something about kissing on a hill – however, the similitude struck me directly.

LYDIA (*aside*). How enraged she'll be presently when she discovers her mistake!

Enter SERVANT.

SERVANT. Sir Anthony and Captain Absolute are below Ma'am.

MRS MALAPROP. Show them up here.

Exit SERVANT.

Now, Lydia, I insist on your behaving as becomes a young woman. Show your good breeding at least, though you have forgot your duty.

LYDIA. Madam, I have told you my resolution; I shall not only give him no encouragement, but I won't even speak to, or look at him.

Flings herself into a chair, with her face from the door.
Enter SIR ANTHONY *and* ABSOLUTE.

SIR ANTHONY. Here we are, Mrs Malaprop; come to mitigate the frowns of unrelenting beauty – and difficulty enough I had to bring this fellow. I don't know what's the matter; but if I hadn't held him by force, he'd have given me the slip.

MRS MALAPROP. You have infinite trouble, Sir Anthony, in the affair. I am ashamed for the cause! (*Aside to her.*) Lydia, Lydia, rise I beseech you! – pay your respects!

SIR ANTHONY. I hope, Madam, that Miss Languish has reflected on the worth of this gentleman, and the regard due to her aunt's choice, and *my* alliance. (*Aside to him.*) Now, Jack, speak to her!

ABSOLUTE (*aside*). What the devil shall I do! – You see, Sir, she
   won't even look at me, whilst you are here. I knew she wouldn't! I
   told you so. Let me entreat you, Sir, to leave us together!

Seems to expostulate with his father.

LYDIA (*aside*). I wonder I ha'n't heard my aunt exclaim yet! sure she
   can't have looked at him! – perhaps their regimentals are alike,
   and she is something blind.

SIR ANTHONY. I say, Sir, I won't stir a foot yet.

MRS MALAPROP. I am sorry to say, Sir Anthony, that my
   affluence over my niece is very small. (*Aside to her.*) Turn round
   Lydia, I blush for you!

SIR ANTHONY. May I not flatter myself that Miss Languish will
   assign what cause of dislike she can have to my son. (*Aside to him.*)
   Why don't you begin, Jack? Speak, you puppy – speak!

MRS MALAPROP. It is impossible, Sir Anthony, she can have any.
   She will not *say* she has. (*Aside to her.*) Answer, hussy! why don't
   you answer?

SIR ANTHONY. Then, Madam, I trust that a childish and hasty
   predilection will be no bar to Jack's happiness. (*Aside to him.*)
   Zounds! sirrah! why don't you speak?

LYDIA. (*Aside.*) I think my lover seems as little inclined to
   conversation as myself. How strangely blind my aunt must be!

ABSOLUTE. Hem! hem! – Madam – hem!

   ABSOLUTE *attempts to speak, then returns to* SIR ANTHONY.

   Faith! Sir, I am so confounded! – and so – so – confused! I told
   you I should be so, Sir – I knew it – the – the – tremor of my
   passion, entirely takes away my presence of mind.

SIR ANTHONY. But it don't take away your voice, fool, does it? Go
   up, and speak to her directly!

   ABSOLUTE *makes signs to* MRS MALAPROP *to leave them together.*

MRS MALAPROP. Sir Anthony, shall we leave them together?

(*Aside to her.*) Ah! you stubborn little vixen!

SIR ANTHONY. Not yet, Ma'am, not yet! (*Aside to him.*) What the devil are you at? Unlock your jaws, sirrah, or –

ABSOLUTE *draws near* LYDIA.

ABSOLUTE. Now heaven send she may be too sullen to look round! (*Aside.*) I must disguise my voice. (*Speaks in a low hoarse tone.*) Will not Miss Languish lend an ear to the mild accents of true love? Will not –

SIR ANTHONY. What the devil ails the fellow? Why don't you speak out? – not stand croaking like a frog in a quinsy!

ABSOLUTE. The – the – excess of my awe, and my – my – my modesty, quite choke me!

SIR ANTHONY. Ah! your *modesty* again! I'll tell you what, Jack; if you don't speak out directly, and glibly too, I shall be in such a rage! Mrs Malaprop, I wish the lady would favour us with something more than a side-front!

MRS MALAPROP *seems to chide* LYDIA.

ABSOLUTE (*aside*). So!   all will out I see! (*Goes up to* LYDIA, *speaks softly.*) Be not surprised, my Lydia, suppress all surprise at present.

LYDIA (*aside*). Heavens! 'tis Beverley's voice! Sure he can't have imposed on Sir Anthony too! (*Looks round by degrees, then starts up.*) Is this possible! – my Beverley! – how can this be? – my Beverley?

ABSOLUTE (*aside*). Ah! 'tis all over.

SIR ANTHONY. Beverley! – the devil – Beverley! – What can the girl mean? This is my son, Jack Absolute!

MRS MALAPROP. For shame, hussy! for shame! – your head runs so on that fellow, that you have him always in your eyes! Beg Captain Absolute's pardon directly.

LYDIA. I see no Captain Absolute, but my loved Beverley!

SIR ANTHONY. Zounds! the girl's mad! – her brain's turned by reading!

MRS MALAPROP. O' my conscience, I believe so! What do you mean by Beverley, hussy? You saw Captain Absolute before today; there he is – your husband that shall be.

LYDIA. With all my soul, Ma'am – when I refuse my Beverley –

SIR ANTHONY. Oh! she's as mad as Bedlam! – or has this fellow been playing us a rogue's trick! Come here, sirrah! Who the devil are you?

ABSOLUTE. Faith, Sir, I am not quite clear myself; but I'll endeavour to recollect.

SIR ANTHONY. Are you my son, or not? Answer for your mother, you dog, if you won't for me.

MRS MALAPROP. Aye, Sir, who are you? O mercy! I begin to suspect –

ABSOLUTE (*aside*). Ye powers of impudence befriend me! – Sir Anthony, most assuredly I am your wife's son; and that I sincerely believe myself to be *yours* also, I hope my duty has always shown. Mrs Malaprop, I am your most respectful admirer – and shall be proud to add *affectionate nephew*. I need not tell my Lydia, that she sees her faithful Beverley, who, knowing the singular generosity of her temper, assumed that name, and a station, which has proved a test of the most disinterested love, which he now hopes to enjoy in a more elevated character.

LYDIA (*sullenly*). So! – there will be no elopement after all!

SIR ANTHONY. Upon my soul, Jack, thou art a very impudent fellow! To do you justice, I think I never saw a piece of more consummate assurance!

ABSOLUTE. Oh, you flatter me, Sir – you compliment – 'tis my *modesty* you know, Sir – my modesty that has stood in my way.

SIR ANTHONY. Well, I am glad you are not the dull, insensible varlet you pretended to be, however! I 'm glad you have made a fool of your father, you dog – I am. – So this was your penitence, your duty, and obedience! I thought it was damned sudden! You never heard their names before, not you! What, Languishes of

Worcestershire, hey? – if you could please me in the affair, 'twas
all you desired! Ah! you dissembling villain! What! (*Pointing to*
LYDIA.) she squints, don't she? – a little red-haired girl! – hey?
Why, you hypocritical young rascal – I wonder you a'n't ashamed
to hold up your head!

ABSOLUTE. 'Tis with much difficulty, Sir – I am confused – very
much confused, as you must perceive.

MRS MALAPROP. O Lud! Sir Anthony! – a new light breaks in
upon me! – hey! how! what! Captain, did you write the letters
then? What! I am to thank you for the elegant compilation of 'an
old weather-beaten she-dragon' – hey? O mercy! – was it you that
reflected on my parts of speech?

ABSOLUTE [*aside to* SIR ANTHONY]. Dear Sir! my modesty will
be overpowered at last, if you don't assist me. I shall certainly not
be able to stand it!

SIR ANTHONY. Come, come, Mrs Malaprop, we must forget and
forgive; odds life! matters have taken so clever a turn all of a
sudden, that I could find it in my heart, to be so goodhumoured!
and so gallant! – hey! Mrs Malaprop!

MRS MALAPROP. Well, Sir Anthony, since you desire it, we will
not anticipate the past; so mind young people – our retrospection
will now be all to the future.

SIR ANTHONY. Come, we must leave them together, Mrs
Malaprop; they long to fly into each other's arms, I warrant!
Jack, isn't the cheek as I said, hey? And the eye, you rogue!
and the lip – hey? Come, Mrs Malaprop, we'll not disturb
their tenderness – theirs is the time of life for happiness! (*Sings.*)
'Youth's the season made for joy' – hey! – odds life! I'm in
such spirits – I don't know what I couldn't do! (*Gives his hand to*
MRS MALAPROP.) Permit me, Ma'am – (*Sings.*) Tol-de-rol –
gad I should like a little fooling myself – tol-de-rol! de-rol!

Exit singing, and handing MRS MALAPROP.

LYDIA *sits sullenly in her chair.*

ABSOLUTE (*aside*). So much thought bodes me no good. – So grave, Lydia!

LYDIA. Sir!

ABSOLUTE (*aside*). So! – egad! I thought as much! – that damned monosyllable has froze me! – What, Lydia, now that we are as happy in our friends' consent as in our mutual vows –

LYDIA (*peevishly*). Friends' consent, indeed!

ABSOLUTE. Come, come, we must lay aside some of our romance – a little wealth and comfort may be endured after all. And for your fortune, the lawyers shall make such settlements as –

LYDIA. Lawyers! I *hate* lawyers!

ABSOLUTE. Nay then, we will not wait for their lingering forms, but instantly procure the licence, and –

LYDIA. The licence! I *hate* licence! ·

ABSOLUTE. O my love! Be not so unkind! – thus let me entreat – (*Kneeling.*)

LYDIA. Pshaw! – what signifies kneeling, when you know I *must* have you?

ABSOLUTE (*rising*). Nay, Madam, there shall be no constraint upon your inclinations, I promise you. If I have lost your *heart* – I resign the rest. (*Aside.*) Gad, I must try what a little *spirit* will do.

LYDIA. (*Rising.*) Then, Sir, let me tell you, the interest you had there was acquired by a mean, unmanly imposition, and deserves the punishment of fraud. What, you have been treating *me* like a *child*! – humouring my romance! and laughing, I suppose, at your success!

ABSOLUTE. You wrong me, Lydia, you wrong me – only hear –

LYDIA (*walking about in heat*). So, while I fondly imagined we were deceiving my relations, and flattered myself that I should outwit and incense them all – behold! my hopes are to be crushed at once, by my aunt's consent and approbation! – and I am myself the only dupe at last!

ABSOLUTE. Nay, but hear me –

LYDIA. No, Sir, you could not think that such paltry artifices could please me, when the mask was thrown off! But I suppose since your tricks have made you secure of my fortune, you are little solicitous about my affections. – But here, Sir, here is the picture – Beverley's picture! (*Taking a miniature from her bosom.*) which I have worn, night and day, in spite of threats and entreaties! There, Sir, (*Flings it to him.*) and be assured I throw the original from my heart as easily!

ABSOLUTE. Nay, nay, Ma'am, we will not differ as to that. Here, (*Taking out a picture.*) *here* is Miss Lydia Languish. What a difference! – aye, there is the heavenly assenting smile, that first gave soul and spirit to my hopes! – those are the lips which sealed a vow, as yet scarce dry in Cupid's calendar! – and there the half resentful blush, that would have checked the ardour of my thanks. – Well, all that's past! – all over indeed! There, Madam – in beauty, that copy is not equal to you, but in my mind its merit over the original, in being still the same, is such – that – I cannot find in my heart to part with it.

Puts it up again.

LYDIA (*softening*). 'Tis your own doing, Sir – I – I – I suppose you are perfectly satisfied.

ABSOLUTE. Oh, most certainly – sure now this is much better than being in love! – ha! ha! ha! – there's some spirit in *this!* What signifies breaking some scores of solemn promises – all that's of no consequence you know. To be sure people will say, that Miss didn't know her own mind – but never mind that: or perhaps they may be ill-natured enough to hint, that the gentleman grew tired of the lady and forsook her – but don't let that fret you.

LYDIA. There's no bearing his insolence.

Bursts into tears. Enter MRS MALAPROP *and* SIR ANTHONY.

MRS MALAPROP (*entering*). Come, we must interrupt your billing and cooing a while.

LYDIA (*sobbing*). This is worse than your treachery and deceit, you base ingrate!

SIR ANTHONY. What the devil's the matter now! Zounds! Mrs Malaprop, this is the oddest *billing* and *cooing* I ever heard! – but what the deuce is the meaning of it? I'm quite astonished!

ABSOLUTE. Ask the lady, Sir.

MRS MALAPROP. O mercy! – I'm quite analysed for my part! Why, Lydia, what is the reason of this?

LYDIA. Ask the gentleman, Ma'am.

SIR ANTHONY. Zounds! I shall be in a frenzy! Why Jack, you scoundrel, you are not come out to be anyone else, are you?

MRS MALAPROP. Aye, Sir, there's no more trick, is there? You are not like Cerberus, *three* gentlemen at once, are you?

ABSOLUTE. You'll not let me speak – I say the lady can account for this much better than I can.

LYDIA. Ma'am, you once commanded me never to think of Beverley again – there is the man – I now obey you: for, from this moment, I renounce him for ever.

Exit LYDIA.

MRS MALAPROP. O mercy! and miracles! what a turn here is – why sure Captain, you haven't behaved disrespectfully to my niece.

SIR ANTHONY. Ha! ha! ha! – ha! ha! ha! – now I see it – ha! ha! ha! – now I see it – you have been too lively, Jack.

ABSOLUTE. Nay, Sir, upon my word –

SIR ANTHONY. Come, no excuses, Jack; why, your father, you rogue, was so before you: the blood of the Absolutes was always impatient. Ha! ha! ha! poor little Lydia! – why, you've frightened her, you dog, you have.

ABSOLUTE. By all that's good, Sir –

SIR ANTHONY. Zounds! say no more, I tell you. Mrs Malaprop
shall make your peace. You must make his peace, Mrs Malaprop;
you must tell her 'tis Jack's way – tell her 'tis all our ways – it runs
in the blood of our family! Come, get on, Jack – ha! ha! ha! Mrs
Malaprop – a young villain!

Pushing him out.

MRS MALAPROP. Oh! Sir Anthony! O fie, Captain!

Exeunt severally.

Scene iii

The North Parade Enter. SIR LUCIUS O'TRIGGER.

SIR LUCIUS. I wonder where this Captain Absolute hides himself.
Upon my conscience! these officers are always in one's way m
love affairs: I remember I might have married Lady Dorothy
Carmine, if it had not been for a little rogue of a Major, who ran
away with her before she could get a sight of me! – And I wonder
too what it is the ladies can see in them to be so fond of them –
unless it be a touch of the old serpent in 'em, that makes the little
creatures be caught, like vipers with a bit of red cloth. – Hah! –
isn't this the Captain coming? Faith it is! There is a probability of
succeeding about that fellow, that is mighty provoking! Who the
devil is he talking to?

Steps aside. Enter CAPTAIN ABSOLUTE.

ABSOLUTE. To what fine purpose I have been plotting! A noble
reward for all my schemes, upon my soul! a little gipsy! I did not
think her romance could have made her so damned absurd
either, 'Sdeath, I never was in a worse humour in my life! I could
cut my own throat, or any other person's with the greatest
pleasure in the world!

SIR LUCIUS. Oh, faith! I'm in the luck of it – I never could have found him in a sweeter temper for my purpose – to be sure I'm just come in the nick! Now to enter into conversation with him, and so quarrel genteelly.

SIR LUCIUS *goes up to* ABSOLUTE.

With regard to that matter, Captain, I must beg leave to differ in opinion with you.

ABSOLUTE. Upon my word then, you must be a very subtle disputant: because, Sir, I happened just then to be giving no opinion at all.

SIR LUCIUS. That's no reason. For give me leave to tell you, a man may think an untruth as well as speak one.

ABSOLUTE. Very true, Sir, but if the man never utters his thoughts, I should think they might stand a chance of escaping controversy.

SIR LUCIUS. Then, Sir, you differ in opinion with me, which amounts to the same thing.

ABSOLUTE. Harkee, Sir Lucius – if I had not before known you to be a gentleman, upon my soul, I should not have discovered it at this interview: for what you can drive at, unless you mean to quarrel with me, I cannot conceive!

SIR LUCIUS (*bowing*). I humbly thank you, Sir, for the quickness of your apprehension – you have named the very thing I would be at.

ABSOLUTE. Very well, Sir – I shall certainly not baulk your inclinations – but I should be glad you would please to explain your motives.

SIR LUCIUS. Pray, Sir, be easy – the quarrel is a very pretty quarrel as it stands – we should only spoil it, by trying to explain it. However, your memory is very short or you could not have forgot an affront you passed on me within this week. So, no more, but name your time and place.

ABSOLUTE. Well, Sir, since you are so bent on it, the sooner the better; let it be this evening – here, by the Spring Gardens. We shall scarcely be interrupted.

SIR LUCIUS. Faith! that same interruption in affairs of this nature shows very great ill-breeding. I don't know what's the reason, but in England, if a thing of this kind gets wind, people make such a pother, that a gentleman can never fight in peace and quietness. However, if it's the same to you, Captain, I should take it as a particular kindness, if you'd let us meet in Kingsmead Fields, as a little business will call me there about six o' clock, and I may dispatch both matters at once.

ABSOLUTE. 'Tis the same to me exactly. A little after six, then, we will discuss this matter more seriously.

SIR LUCIUS. If you please, Sir, there will be very pretty small-sword light, though it won't do for a long shot. – So that matter's settled! and my mind's at ease.

Exit SIR LUCIUS. *Enter* FAULKLAND, *meeting* ABSOLUTE.

ABSOLUTE. Well met – I was going to look for you. O Faulkland! all the demons of spite and disappointment have conspired against me! I'm so vexed, that if I had not the prospect of a resource in being knocked o'the head by and by, I should scarce have spirits to tell you the cause.

FAULKLAND. What can you mean? Has Lydia changed her mind? I should have thought her duty and inclination would now have pointed to the same object.

ABSOLUTE. Aye, just as the eyes do of a person who squints: when her love eye was fixed on me – t'other, her eye of duty, was finely obliged: but when duty bid her point that the same way, off t'other turned on a swivel, and secured its retreat with a frown!

FAULKLAND. But what's the resource you –

ABSOLUTE. Oh, to wind up the whole, a good-natured Irishman here has (*Mimicking* SIR LUCIUS.) begged leave to have the pleasure of cutting my throat – and I mean to indulge him – that's all.

FAULKLAND. Prithee, be serious.

ABSOLUTE. 'Tis fact, upon my soul. Sir Lucius O'Trigger – you know him by sight – for some affront, which I am sure I never intended, has obliged me to meet him this evening at six o'clock: 'tis on that account I wished to see you – you must go with me.

FAULKLAND. Nay, there must be some mistake, sure. Sir Lucius shall explain himself and I dare say matters may be accommodated: but this evening, did you say? I wish it had been any other time.

ABSOLUTE. Why? – there will be light enough: there will (as Sir Lucius says) 'be very pretty small-sword light, though it won't do for a long shot'. Confound his long shots!

FAULKLAND. But I am myself a good deal ruffled, by a difference I have had with Julia – my vile tormenting temper had made me treat her so cruelly, that I shall not be myself till we are reconciled.

ABSOLUTE. By heavens, Faulkland, you don't deserve her.

Enter SERVANT, *gives* FAULKLAND *a letter.* [*Exit* SERVANT.]

FAULKLAND. O Jack! this is from Julia – I dread to open it – I fear it may be to take a last leave – perhaps to bid me return her letters – and restore – oh! how I suffer for my folly!

ABSOLUTE. Here – let me see. (*Takes the letter and opens it.*) Aye, a final sentence indeed! – 'tis all over with you, faith!

FAULKLAND. Nay, Jack don't keep me in suspense.

ABSOLUTE. Hear then. '*As I am convinced that my dear Faulkland's own reflections have already upbraided him for his last unkindness to me, I will not add a word on the subject. I wish to speak with you as soon as possible. Yours ever and truly, Julia.*' – There's stubbornness and resentment for you! (*Gives him the letter.*) Why, man, you don't seem one whit the happier at this.

FAULKLAND. Oh, yes, I am – but – but –

ABSOLUTE. Confound your buts. You never hear anything that
would make another man bless himself, but you immediately
damn it with a but.

FAULKLAND. Now, Jack, as you are my friend, own honestly –
don't you think there is something forward – something indelicate
in this haste to forgive? Women should never sue for reconcili-
ation: that should *always* come from us. They should retain their
coldness till wooed to kindness – and their pardon, like their love,
should 'not unsought be won'.

ABSOLUTE. I have not patience to listen to you: thou'rt
incorrigible! – so say no more on the subject. I must go to settle a
few matters – let me see you before six – remember – at my
lodgings. A poor industrious devil like me, who have toiled, and
drudged, and plotted to gain my ends, and am at last
disappointed by other people's folly – may in pity be allowed to
swear and grumble a little; but a captious sceptic in love – a slave
to fretfulness and whim – who has no difficulties but of his own
creating – is a subject more fit for ridicule than compassion!

Exit ABSOLUTE

FAULKLAND. I feel his reproaches! Yet I would not change this too
exquisite nicety, for the gross content with which he tramples on
the thorns of love. His engaging me in this duel has started an
idea in my head, which I will instantly pursue. I'll use it as the
touchstone of Julia's sincerity and disinterestedness – if her love
prove pure and sterling ore – my name will rest on it with
honour! And once I've stamped it there, I lay aside my doubts
for ever: but if the dross of selfishness, the allay of pride predomi-
nate – 'twill be best to leave her as a toy for some less cautious
fool to sigh for.

Exit FAULKLAND.

Act V, Scene i

JULIA'S *dressing-room.* JULIA, *sola.*

JULIA. How this message has alarmed me! what dreadful accident
can he mean! why such charge to be alone? O Faulkland! how
many unhappy moments! how many tears have you cost me!

Enter FAULKLAND, *muffled up in a riding coat.*

JULIA. What means this? – Why this caution, Faulkland?

FAULKLAND. Alas! Julia, I am come to take a long farewell.

JULIA. Heavens! what do you mean?

FAULKLAND. You see before you a wretch, whose life is forfeited.
Nay, start not! The infirmity of my temper has drawn all this
misery on me. I left you fretful and passionate – an untoward
accident drew me into a quarrel – the event is, that I must fly this
kingdom instantly. O Julia, had I been so fortunate as to have
called you mine entirely, before this mischance had fallen on me,
I should not so deeply dread my banishment!

JULIA. My soul is oppressed with sorrow at the nature of your
misfortune: had these adverse circumstances arisen from a less
fatal cause, I should have felt strong comfort in the thought that
I could *now* chase from your bosom every doubt of the warm
sincerity of my love. My heart has long known no other guardian
– I now entrust my person to your honour – we will fly together.
When safe from pursuit, my father's will may be fulfilled – and
I receive a legal claim to be the partner of your sorrows, and
tenderest comforter. Then on the bosom of your wedded Julia,
you may lull your keen regret to slumbering; while virtuous love,
with a cherub's hand, shall smooth the brow of upbraiding
thought, and pluck the thorn from compunction.

FAULKLAND. O Julia! I am bankrupt in gratitude! but the time is so pressing, it calls on you for so hasty a resolution. Would you not wish some hours to weigh the advantages you forego, and what little compensation poor Faulkland can make you beside his solitary love?

JULIA. I ask not a moment. No, Faulkland, I have loved you for yourself: and if I now, more than ever, prize the solemn engagement which so long has pledged us to each other, it is because it leaves no room for hard aspersions on my fame, and puts the seal of duty to an act of love. But let us not linger – perhaps this delay –

FAULKLAND. 'Twill be better I should not venture out again till dark. Yet am I grieved to think what numberless distresses will press heavy on your gentle disposition!

JULIA. Perhaps your fortune may be forfeited by this unhappy act. I know not whether 'tis so – but sure that alone can never make us unhappy. The little I have will be sufficient to support us; and exile never should be splendid.

FAULKLAND. Aye, but in such an abject state of life, my wounded pride perhaps may increase the natural fretfulness of my temper, till I become a rude, morose companion, beyond your patience to endure. Perhaps the recollection of a deed my conscience cannot justify, may haunt me in such gloomy and unsocial fits, that I shall hate the tenderness that would relieve me, break from your arms, and quarrel with your fondness!

JULIA. If your thoughts should assume so unhappy a bent, you will the more want some mild and affectionate spirit to watch over and console you: one who, by bearing your infirmities with gentleness and resignation, may teach you so to bear the evils of your fortune.

FAULKLAND. O Julia, I have proved you to the quick! and with this useless device I throw away all my doubts. How shall I plead to be forgiven this last unworthy effect of my restless, unsatisfied disposition?

JULIA. Has no such disaster happened as you related?

FAULKLAND. I am ashamed to own that it was all pretended; yet, in pity, Julia, do not kill me with resenting a fault which never can be repeated: but sealing, this once, my pardon, let me tomorrow, in the face of heaven, receive my future guide and monitress, and expiate my past folly, by years of tender adoration.

JULIA. Hold, Faulkland! That you are free from a crime, which I before feared to name, heaven knows how sincerely I rejoice! These are tears of thankfulness for that! But that your cruel doubts should have urged you to an imposition that has wrung my heart, gives me now a pang, more keen than I can express!

FAULKLAND. By heavens! Julia –

JULIA. Yet hear me. – My father loved you, Faulkland! and you preserved the life that tender parent gave me; in his presence I pledged my hand – joyfully pledged it – where before I had given my heart. When, soon after, I lost that parent, it seemed to me that providence had, in Faulkland shown me whither to transfer, without a pause, my grateful duty, as well as my affection. Hence I have been content to bear from you what pride and delicacy would have forbid me from another. I will not upbraid you, by repeating how you have trifled with my sincerity –

FAULKLAND. I confess it all! yet hear –

JULIA. After such a year of trial – I might have flattered myself that I should not have been insulted with a new probation of my sincerity, as cruel as unnecessary! I now see it is not in your nature to be content, or confident in love. With this conviction – I never will be yours. While I had hopes that my persevering attention, and unreproaching kindness might in time reform your temper, I should have been happy to have gained a dearer influence over you; but I will not furnish you with a licensed power to keep alive an incorrigible fault, at the expense of one who never would contend with you.

FAULKLAND. Nay, but Julia, by my soul and honour, if after this –

JULIA. But one word more. As my faith has once been given to you, I never will barter it with another. I shall pray for your happiness with the truest sincerity, and the dearest blessing I can ask of heaven to send you, will be to charm you from that unhappy temper, which alone has prevented the performance of our solemn engagement. All I request of you is, that you will yourself reflect upon this infirmity, and when you number up the many true delights it has deprived you of – let it not be your *least* regret, that it lost you the love of one – who would have followed you in beggary through the world!

Exit.

FAULKLAND. She's gone! – for ever! There was an awful resolution in her manner, that riveted me to my place. – O fool! – dolt! – barbarian! Curst as I am, with more imperfections than my fellow-wretches, kind fortune sent a heaven-gifted cherub to my aid, and, like a ruffian, I have driven her from my side! I must now haste to my appointment. Well, my mind is tuned for such a scene. I shall wish only to become a principal in it, and reverse the tale my cursed folly put me upon forging here. O love! – tormentor! – fiend! – whose influence, like the moon's, acting on men of dull souls, makes idiots of them, but meeting subtler spirits, betrays their course, and urges sensibility to madness!

Exit. Enter MAID *and* LYDIA.

MAID My mistress, Ma'am, I know, was here just now – perhaps she is only in the next room.

Exit MAID.

LYDIA. Heigh ho! – though he has used me so, this fellow runs strangely in my head. I believe one lecture from my grave cousin will make me recall him.

Enter JULIA.

LYDIA. O Julia, I am come to you with such an appetite for consolation. Lud! child, what's the matter with you? You have been crying! I'll be hanged, if that Faulkland has not been tormenting you!

JULIA. You mistake the cause of my uneasiness – something *has* flurried me a little – nothing that you can guess at. – (*Aside.*)

I would not accuse Faulkland to a sister!

LYDIA. Ah! whatever vexations you may have, I can assure you mine surpass them. You know who Beverley proves to be?

JULIA. I will now own to you, Lydia, that Mr Faulkland had before informed me of the whole affair. Had young Absolute been the person you took him for, I should not have accepted your confidence on the subject, without a serious endeavour to counteract your caprice.

LYDIA. So, then, I see I have been deceived by everyone! – but I don't care – I'll never have him.

JULIA. Nay, Lydia

LYDIA. Why, is it not provoking; when I thought we were coming to the prettiest distress imaginable, to find myself made a mere Smithfield bargain of at last. – There had I projected one of the most sentimental elopements! – so becoming a disguise! – so amiable a ladder of ropes! – conscious moon – four horses – Scotch parson – with such surprise to Mrs Malaprop – and such paragraphs in the newspapers! – Oh, I shall die with disappointment.

JULIA. I don't wonder at it!

LYDIA. Now – sad reverse! – what have I to expect, but, after a deal of flimsy preparation with a bishop's licence, and my aunt's blessing, to go simpering up to the altar; or perhaps be cried three times in a country church, and have an unmannerly fat clerk ask the consent of every butcher in the parish to join John Absolute and Lydia Languish *spinster!* Oh, that I should live to hear myself called spinster!

JULIA. Melancholy, indeed!

LYDIA. How mortifying, to remember the dear delicious shifts I used to be put to, to gain half a minute's conversation with this fellow! How often have I stole forth, in the coldest night in January, and found him in the garden, stuck like a dripping statue! There would he kneel to me in the snow, and sneeze and cough so pathetically! he shivering with cold, and I with apprehension! and while the freezing blast numbed our joints, how warmly would he press me to pity his flame, and glow with mutual ardour! – Ah, Julia! that was something like being in love.

JULIA. If I were in spirits, Lydia, I should chide you only by laughing heartily at you: but it suits more the situation of my mind, at present, earnestly to entreat you, not to let a man, who loves you with sincerity, suffer that unhappiness from your caprice, which I know too well caprice can infllct.

LYDIA. O Lud! what has brought my aunt here!

Enter MRS MALAPROP, FAG, *and* DAVID.

MRS MALAPROP. So! so! Here's fine work! Here's fine suicide, paracide, and simulation going on in the fields! and Sir Anthony not to be found to prevent the antistrophe!

JULIA. For heaven's sake, Madam, what's the meaning of this?

MRS MALAPROP. That gentleman can tell you – 'twas he enveloped the affair to me.

LYDIA (*to* FAG). Do, Sir, will you inform us.

FAG. Ma'am, I should hold myself very deficient in every requisite that forms the man of breeding, if I delayed a moment to give all the information in my power to a lady so deeply interested in the affair as you are.

LYDIA. But quick! quick, Sir!

FAG. True, Ma'am, as you say, one should be quick in divulging matters of this nature; for should we be tedious, perhaps while we are flourishing on the subject, two or three lives may be lost!

LYDIA. O patience! Do, Ma'am, for heaven's sake! tell us what is the matter?

MRS MALAPROP. Why, murder's the matter! slaughter's the matter! killing's the matter! – but he can tell you the perpendiculars.

LYDIA. Then, prithee, Sir, be brief.

FAG. Why then, Ma'am as to murder – I cannot take upon me to say – and as to slaughter, or manslaughter, that will be as the jury finds it.

LYDIA. But who, Sir – who are engaged in this?

FAG. Faith, Ma'am, one is a young gentleman whom I should be very sorry anything was to happen to – a very pretty behaved gentleman! We have lived much together, and always on terms.

LYDIA. But who is this? who! who! who!

FAG. My master, Ma'am – my master – I speak of my master.

LYDIA. Heavens! What, Captain Absolute!

MRS MALAPROP. Oh, to be sure, you are frightened now!

JULIA. But who are with him, Sir?

FAG. As to the rest, Ma'am, this gentleman can inform you better than I.

JULIA (*to* DAVID). Do speak, friend.

DAVID. Lookee, my lady – by the mass! there's mischief going on. – Folks don't use to meet for amusement with firearms, firelocks, fire-engines, fire-screens, fire-office, and the devil knows what other crackers besides! – This, my lady, I say, has an angry favour.

JULIA. But who is there beside Captain Absolute, friend?

DAVID. My poor master – under favour, for mentioning him first. You know me, my lady – I am David and my master of course is, or *was*, Squire Acres. Then comes Squire Faulkland.

JULIA. Do, Ma'am, let us instantly endeavour to prevent mischief.

MRS MALAPROP. O fie – it would be very inelegant in us: we should only participate things.

DAVID. Ah! do, Mrs Aunt, save a few lives – they are desperately given, believe me. Above all, there is that bloodthirsty Philistine, Sir Lucius O'Trigger.

MRS MALAPROP. Sir Lucius O'Trigger! O mercy! have they drawn poor little dear Sir Lucius into the scrape? Why, how, how you stand, girl! you have no more feeling than one of the Derbyshire putrefactions!

LYDIA. What are we to do, Madam?

MRS MALAPROP. Why, fly with the utmost felicity to be sure, to prevent mischief: here, friend – you can show us the place?

FAG. If you please, Ma'am, I will conduct you. David, do you look for Sir Anthony.

Exit DAVID.

MRS MALAPROP. Come, girls! this gentleman will exhort us. Come, Sir, you're our envoy – lead the way, and we'll precede.

FAG. Not a step before the ladies for the world!

MRS MALAPROP. You're sure you know the spot.

FAG. I think I can find it, Ma'am; and one good thing is, we shall hear the report of the pistols as we draw near, so we can't well miss them; never fear, Ma'am, never fear.

Exeunt, he talking.

Scene ii

South Parade. Enter ABSOLUTE, *putting his sword under his greatcoat.*

ABSOLUTE. A sword seen in the streets of Bath would raise as great an alarm as a mad dog. How provoking this is in Faulkland! – never punctual! I shall be obliged to go without him at last. Oh, the devil! here's Sir Anthony! – how shall I escape him?

Muffles up his face, and takes a circle to go off. Enter SIR ANTHONY.

SIR ANTHONY. How one may be deceived at a little distance! Only that I see he don't know me, I could have sworn that was Jack! Hey! Gad's life, it is. Why, Jack, you dog! what are you afraid of? Hey! sure I'm right. Why, Jack – Jack Absolute!

Goes up to him.

ABSOLUTE. Really, Sir, you have the advantage of me: I don't remember ever to have had the honour – my name is Saunderson, at your service.

SIR ANTHONY. Sir, I beg your pardon – I took you – hey! – why, zounds! it is – stay – (*Looks up to his face.*) So, so – your humble servant, Mr Saunderson! Why, you scoundrel, what tricks are you after now?

ABSOLUTE. Oh! a joke, Sir, a joke! I came here on purpose to look for you, Sir.

SIR ANTHONY. You did! Well, I am glad you were so lucky: but what are you muffled up so for? What's this for? – hey?

ABSOLUTE. 'Tis cool, Sir; isn't it? – rather chilly somehow: but I shall be late – I have a particular engagement.

SIR ANTHONY. Stay – why, I thought you were looking for me? Pray, Jack, where is't you are going?

ABSOLUTE. Going, Sir!

SIR ANTHONY. Aye – where are you going?

ABSOLUTE. Where am I going?

SIR ANTHONY. You unmannerly puppy!

ABSOLUTE. I was going, Sir, to – to – to – to Lydia – Sir to Lydia – to make matters up if I could; and I was looking for you, Sir, to – to –

SIR ANTHONY. To go with you, I suppose – well, come along.

ABSOLUTE. Oh! zounds! no, Sir, not for the world! I wished to meet with you, Sir, to – to – to – you find it cool, I'm sure Sir – you'd better not stay out.

SIR ANTHONY. Cool! not at all – well, Jack – and what will you say to Lydia?

ABSOLUTE. Oh, Sir, beg her pardon, humour her – promise and vow: but I detain you, Sir – consider the cold air on your gout.

SIR ANTHONY. Oh, not at all! – not at all! – I'm in no hurry. Ah! Jack, you youngsters when once you are wounded here. (*Putting his hand to* ABSOLUTE's *breast.*) Hey! what the deuce have you got here?

ABSOLUTE. Nothing, Sir – nothing.

SIR ANTHONY. What's this? – here's something damned hard!

ABSOLUTE. Oh, trinkets, Sir! trinkets – a bauble for Lydia!

SIR ANTHONY. Nay let me see your taste. (*Pulls his coat open, the sword falls.*) Trinkets! – a bauble for Lydia! Zounds! sirrah, you are not going to cut her throat, are you?

ABSOLUTE. Ha! ha! ha! – I thought it would divert you, Sir, though I didn't mean to tell you till afterwards.

SIR ANTHONY. You didn't? Yes, this is a very diverting trinket, truly.

ABSOLUTE. Sir, I'll explain to you. You know, Sir, Lydia is romantic devilish romantic, and very absurd of course: now Sir, I intend, if she refuses to forgive me – to unsheath this sword – and swear – I'll fall upon its point, and expire at her feet!

SIR ANTHONY. Fall upon a fiddlestick's end! Why, I suppose it is the very thing that would please her. Get along, you fool.

ABSOLUTE. Well, Sir, you shall hear of my success – you shall hear.'Oh, Lydia! forgive me, or this pointed steel' says I.

SIR ANTHONY. 'Oh, booby! stab away, and welcome' – says she. Get along! and damn your trinkets!

Exit ABSOLUTE. *Enter* DAVID, *running.*

DAVID. Stop him! stop him! murder! thief! fire! Stop fire! stop fire! Oh! Sir Anthony call! call! bid 'em stop! Murder!Fire!

SIR ANTHONY. Fire! murder! where?

DAVID. Oons! he's out of sight! and I 'm out of breath, for my part! Oh, Sir Anthony, why didn't you stop him? why didn't you stop him?

SIR ANTHONY. Zounds! the fellow's mad! – Stop whom? Stop Jack?

DAVID. Aye, the Captain, Sir! – there's murder and slaughter –

SIR ANTHONY. Murder!

DAVID. Aye, please you, Sir Anthony, there's all kinds of murder, all sorts of slaughter to be seen in the fields: there's fighting going on, Sir – bloody sword-and-gun fighting!

SIR ANTHONY. Who are going to fight, dunce?

DAVID. Everybody that I know of, Sir Anthony: everybody is going to fight, my poor master, Sir Lucius O'Trigger, your son, the Captain –

SIR ANTHONY. Oh, the dog! I see his tricks – do you know the place?

DAVID. Kingsmead Fields.

SIR ANTHONY. You know the way?

DAVID. Not an inch; but I'll call the mayor – aldermen – constables – churchwardens – and beadles – we can't be too many to part them.

SIR ANTHONY. Come along – give me your shoulder! We'll get assistance as we go – the lying villain! Well, I shall be in such a frenzy– so – this was the history of his damned trinkets! I'll bauble him!

Exeunt.

Scene iii

Kingsmead Fields. SIR LUCIUS *and* ACRES, *with pistols.*

ACRES. By my valour! then, Sir Lucius, forty yards is a good distance – odds levels and aims! I say it is a good distance.

SIR LUCIUS. Is it for muskets or small field-pieces? Upon my conscience, Mr Acres, you must leave those things to me. Stay now – I'll show you. (*Measures paces along the stage.*) There now, that is a very pretty distance – a pretty gentleman's distance.

ACRES. Zounds! we might as well fight in a sentry-box! I tell you, Sir Lucius, the farther he is off, the cooler I shall take my aim.

SIR LUCIUS. Faith! then I suppose you would aim at him best of all if he was out of sight!

ACRES. No, Sir Lucius – but I should think forty or eight and thirty yards –

SIR LUCIUS. Pho! pho! nonsense! Three or four feet between the mouths of your pistols is as good as a mile.

ACRES. Odds bullets, no! – by my valour! there is no merit in killing him so near: do, my dear Sir Lucius, let me bring him down at a long shot: a long shot, Sir Lucius, if you love me!

SIR LUCIUS. Well – the gentleman's friend and I must settle that. But tell me now, Mr Acres, in case of an accident, is there any little will or commission I could execute for you?

ACRES. I am much obliged to you, Sir Lucius – but I don't understand –

SIR LUCIUS. Why, you may think there's no being shot at without a little risk – and if an unlucky bullet should carry a quietus with it – I say it will be no time then to be bothering you about family matters.

ACRES. A *quietus*!

SIR LUCIUS. For instance now – if that should be the case – would you choose to be pickled and sent home? or would it be the same to you to lie here in the Abbey? I'm told there is very snug lying in the Abbey.

ACRES. Pickled! Snug lying in the Abbey! Odds tremors! Sir Lucius, don't talk so!

SIR LUCIUS. I suppose, Mr Acres, you never were engaged in an affair of this kind before?

ACRES. No, Sir Lucius, never before.

SIR LUCIUS. Ah! that's a pity! – there's nothing like being used to a thing. Pray now, how would you receive the gentleman's shot?

ACRES. Odds files! I've practised that – there, Sir Lucius – there (*Puts himself in an attitude.*) – a side-front, hey? Odd! I'll make myself small enough – I'll stand edge-ways.

SIR LUCIUS. Now – you're quite out – for if you stand so when I take my aim –

Levelling at him

ACRES. Zounds! Sir Lucius – are you sure it is not cocked?

SIR LUCIUS. Never fear.

ACRES. But – but – you don't know – it may go off of its own head!

SIR LUCIUS. Pho! be easy. Well, now if I hit you in the body, my bullet has a double chance – for if it misses a vital part on your right side – 'twill be very hard if it don't succeed on the left!

ACRES. A vital part! Oh, my poor vitals!

SIR LUCIUS. But, there – fix yourself so – (*Placing him.*) let him see the broad side of your full front – there – now a ball or two may pass clean through your body, and never do any harm at all.

ACRES. Clean through me! – a ball or two clean through me!

SIR LUCIUS. Aye – may they – and it is much the genteelest attitude into the bargain.

ACRES. Lookee! Sir Lucius – I 'd just as lief be shot in an awkward posture as a genteel one – so, by my valour! I will stand edgeways.

SIR LUCIUS (*looking at his watch*). Sure they don't mean to
disappoint us. Hah? No, faith – I think I see them coming.

ACRES. Hey! – what! – coming!

SIR LUCIUS. Aye – who are those yonder getting over the stile?

ACRES. There are two of them, indeed! Well – let them come – hey,
Sir Lucius! – we – we – we – we – won't run.

SIR LUCIUS. Run!

ACRES. No – I say – we *won't* run, by my valour!

SIR LUCIUS. What the devil's the matter with you?

ACRES. Nothing – nothing – my dear friend – my dear Sir Lucius –
but – I – I – I don't feel quite so bold, somehow – as I did.

SIR LUCIUS. O fie! consider your honour.

ACRES. Aye – true – my honour – do, Sir Lucius, hedge in a word
or two every now and then about my honour.

SIR LUCIUS (*looking*). Well, here they're coming.

ACRES. Sir Lucius – if I wa'n't with you, I should almost think I was
afraid – if my valour should leave me! – Valour will come and go.

SIR LUCIUS. Then pray keep it fast, while you have it.

ACRES. Sir Lucius – I doubt it is going – yes – my valour is certainly
going! – it is sneaking off! I feel it oozing out as it were at the
palms of my hands!

SIR LUCIUS. Your honour – your honour – here they are.

ACRES. O mercy! – now – that I were safe at Clod Hall! or could be
shot before I was aware!

Enter FAULKLAND *and* ABSOLUTE.

SIR LUCIUS. Gentlemen, your most obedient – hah! – what
Captain Absolute! So, I suppose, Sir, you are come here, just like
myself – to do a kind office, first for your friend – then to proceed
to business on your own account.

ACRES. What, Jack! – my dear Jack! – my dear friend!

ABSOLUTE. Harkee, Bob, Beverley's at hand.

SIR LUCIUS. Well, Mr Acres – I don't blame your saluting the gentleman civilly. So, Mr Beverley, (*To* FAULKLAND.) if you'll choose your weapons, the Captain and I will measure the ground.

FAULKLAND. *My* weapons, Sir.

ACRES. Odds life! Sir Lucius, I'm not going to fight Mr Faulkland; these are my particular friends.

SIR LUCIUS. What, Sir, did you not come here to fight Mr Acres?

FAULKLAND Not I, upon my word, Sir.

SIR LUCIUS. Well, now, that's mighty provoking! But I hope, Mr Faulkland, as there are three of us come on purpose for the game, you won't be so cantankerous as to spoil the party by sitting out.

ABSOLUTE. O pray, Faulkland, fight to oblige Sir Lucius.

FAULKLAND. Nay, if Mr Acres is so bent on the matter.

ACRES. No, no, Mr Faulkland – I'll bear my disappointment like a Christian. Lookee, Sir Lucius, there's no occasion at all for me to fight; and if it is the same to you, I'd as lief let it alone.

SIR LUCIUS. Observe me, Mr Acres – I must not be trifled with. You have certainly challenged somebody – and you came here to fight him. Now, if that gentleman is willing to represent him – I can't see, for my soul, why it isn't just the same thing.

ACRES. Why no – Sir Lucius – I tell you, 'tis one Beverley I've challenged – a fellow, you see, that dare not show his face! if *he* were here, I'd make him give up his pretensions directly!

ABSOLUTE. Hold, Bob – let me set you right – there is no such man as Beverley in the case. The person who assumed that name is before you; and as his pretensions are the same in both characters, he is ready to support them in whatever way you please.

SIR LUCIUS. Well, this is lucky – now you have an opportunity –

ACRES. What, quarrel with my dear friend Jack Absolute – not if he were fifty Beverleys! Zounds! Sir Lucius, you would not have me be so unnatural.

SIR LUCIUS. Upon my conscience, Mr Acres, your valour has oozed away with a vengeance!

ACRES. Not in the least! Odds backs and abettors! I'll be your second with all my heart – and if you should get a quietus, you may command me entirely. I'll get you a snug lying in the Abbey here; or pickle you, and send you over to Blunderbuss Hall, or anything of the kind with the greatest pleasure.

SIR LUCIUS. Pho! pho! you are little better than a coward.

ACRES. Mind, gentlemen, he calls me a coward; coward was the word, by my valour!

SIR LUCIUS. Well, Sir?

ACRES. Lookee, Sir Lucius, 'tisn't that I mind the word coward – coward may be said in joke. But if you had called me a poltroon, odds daggers and balls!

SIR LUCIUS. Well, Sir?

ACRES. – I should have thought you a very ill-bred man.

SIR LUCIUS. Pho! you are beneath my notice.

ABSOLUTE. Nay, Sir Lucius, you can't have a better second than my friend, Acres. He is a most determined dog – called in the country, 'Fighting Bob'. He generally kills a man a week; don't you, Bob?

ACRES. Aye – at home!

SIR LUCIUS. Well then, Captain, 'tis we must begin – so come out, my little counsellor, (*Draws his sword.*) and ask the gentleman, whether he will resign the lady, without forcing you to proceed against him?

ABSOLUTE. Come on then, Sir; (*Draws.*) since you won't let it be an amicable suit, here's my reply.

Enter SIR ANTHONY, DAVID, [MRS MALAPROP, LYDIA, *and* JULIA].

DAVID. Knock 'em down, sweet Sir Anthony, knock down my master in particular – and bind his hands over to their good behaviour!

SIR ANTHONY. Put up, Jack, put up, or I shall be in a frenzy – how came you in a duel, Sir?

ABSOLUTE. Faith, Sir, that gentleman can tell you better than I; 'twas he called on me, and you know, Sir, I serve his Majesty.

SIR ANTHONY. Here's a pretty fellow, I catch him going to cut a man's throat, and he tells me, he serves his Majesty! – Zounds! sirrah, then how durst you draw the King's sword against one of his subjects?

ABSOLUTE. Sir, I tell you! That gentleman called me out, without explaining his reasons.

SIR ANTHONY. Gad! Sir, how came you to call my son out, without explaining your reasons?

SIR LUCIUS. Your son, Sir, insulted me in a manner which my honour could not brook.

SIR ANTHONY. Zounds! Jack, how durst you insult the gentleman in a manner which his honour could not brook?

MRS MALAPROP. Come, come, let's have no honour before ladies. Captain Absolute, come here – how could you intimidate us so? Here's Lydia has been terrified to death for you.

ABSOLUTE. For fear I should be killed, or escape, Ma'am?

MRS MALAPROP. Nay, no delusions to the past – Lydia is convinced; speak child.

SIR LUCIUS. With your leave, Ma'am, I must put in a word here – I believe I could interpret the young lady's silence. Now mark –

LYDIA. What is it you mean, Sir?

SIR LUCIUS. Come, come, Delia, we must be serious now – this is no time for trifling.

LYDIA. 'Tis true, Sir; and your reproof bids me offer this gentleman my hand, and solicit the return of his affections.

ABSOLUTE. Oh! my little angel, say you so? – Sir Lucius, I perceive there must be some mistake here – with regard to the affront which you affirm I have given you – I can only say, that it could not have been intentional. And as you must be convinced, that I should not fear to support a real injury – you shall now see that I am not ashamed to atone for an inadvertency – I ask your pardon. But for this lady, while honoured with her approbation, I will support my claim against any man whatever.

SIR ANTHONY. Well said, Jack, and I'll stand by you, my boy.

ACRES. Mind, I give up all my claim – I make no pretensions to anything in the world – and if I can't get a wife, without fighting for her, by my valour! I'll live a bachelor.

SIR LUCIUS. Captain, give me your hand – an affront handsomely acknowledged becomes an obligation – and as for the lady – if she chooses to deny her own handwriting here –

Taking out letters.

MRS MALAPROP. Oh, he will dissolve my mystery! Sir Lucius, perhaps there's some mistake – perhaps, I can illuminate –

SIR LUCIUS. Pray, old gentlewoman, don't interfere, where you have no business. Miss Languish, are you my Delia, or not?

LYDIA. Indeed, Sir Lucius, I am not.

LYDIA *and* ABSOLUTE *walk aside.*

MRS MALAPROP. Sir Lucius O'Trigger – ungrateful as you are – I own the soft impeachment – pardon my blushes, I am Delia.

SIR LUCIUS. You Delia – pho! pho! be easy.

MRS MALAPROP. Why, thou barbarous Vandyke – those letters are mine. When you are more sensible of my benignity – perhaps

I may be brought to encourage your addresses.

SIR LUCIUS. Mrs Malaprop, I am extremely sensible of your condescension; and whether you or Lucy have put this trick upon me, I am equally beholden to you. And to show you I'm not ungrateful, Captain Absolute! since you have taken that lady from me, I'll give you my Delia into the bargain.

ABSOLUTE. I am much obliged to you, Sir Lucius, but here's our friend, Fighting Bob, unprovided for.

SIR LUCIUS. Hah! little Valour – here, will you make your fortune?

ACRES. Odds wrinkles! No. But give me your hand, Sir Lucius, forget and forgive; but if ever I give you a chance of pickling me again, say Bob Acres is a dunce, that's all.

SIR ANTHONY. Come, Mrs Malaprop, don't be cast down – you are in your bloom yet.

MRS MALAPROP. O Sir Anthony! – men are all barbarians –

All retire but JULIA *and* FAULKLAND.

JULIA. He seems dejected and unhappy – not sullen – there was some foundation, however, for the tale he told me – O woman! how true should be your judgment, when your resolution is so weak!

FAULKLAND. Julia! – how can I sue for what I so little deserve? I dare not presume – yet hope is the child of penitence.

JULIA. Oh! Faulkland, you have not been more faulty in your unkind treatment of me, than I am now in wanting inclination to resent it. As my heart honestly bids me place my weakness to the account of love, I should be ungenerous not to admit the same plea for yours.

FAULKLAND. Now I shall be blest indeed!

SIR ANTHONY *comes forward.*

SIR ANTHONY. What's going on here? So you have been quarrelling too, I warrant. Come, Julia, I never interfered before;

but let me have a hand in the matter at last. All the faults I have ever seen in my friend Faulkland, seemed to proceed from what he calls the *delicacy* and *warmth* of his affection for you – there. marry him directly, Julia, you'll find he'll mend surprisingly!

The rest come forward.

SIR LUCIUS. Come now, I hope there is no dissatisfied person, but what is content; for as I have been disappointed myself, it will be very hard if I have not the satisfaction of seeing other people succeed better –

ACRES. You are right, Sir Lucius. So, Jack, I wish you joy – Mr Faulkland the same. Ladies, come now, to show you I'm neither vexed nor angry, odds tabors and pipes! I'll order the fiddles in half an hour, to the New Rooms – and I insist on your all meeting me there.

SIR ANTHONY. Gad! Sir, I like your spirit; and at night we single lads will drink a health to the young couples, and a husband to Mrs Malaprop.

FAULKLAND. Our partners are stolen from us, Jack – I hope to be congratulated by each other – yours for having checked in time the errors of an ill-directed imagination, which might have betrayed an innocent heart; and mine, for having, by her gentleness and candour, reformed the unhappy temper of one, who by it made wretched whom he loved most, and tortured the heart he ought to have adored.

ABSOLUTE. Well, Faulkland, we have both tasted the bitters, as well as the sweets, of love – with this difference only, that you always prepared the bitter cup for yourself, while I –

LYDIA. Was always obliged to me for it, hey! Mr Modesty? – But come, no more of that – our happiness is now as unallayed as general.

JULIA. Then let us study to preserve it so: and while hope pictures to us a flattering scene of future bliss, let us deny its pencil those colours which are too bright to be lasting. When hearts deserving happiness would unite their fortunes, virtue would crown them with an unfading garland of modest, hurtless flowers; but ill-judging passion will force the gaudier rose into the wreath, whose thorn offends them, when its leaves are dropped!

Finis.

Epilogue

By the author.

Spoken by Mrs Bulkley.

Ladies for you – I heard our poet say –
He'd try to coax some moral from his play:
'One moral's plain' – cried I – 'without more fuss
Man's social happiness all rests on us –
Through all the drama – whether damned or not –
Love gilds the scene, and women guide the plot.
From every rank obedience is our due –
D'ye doubt? – the world's great stage shall prove it true'.
The cit – well skilled to shun domestic strife –
Will sup abroad; but first – he'll ask his wife:
John Trot, his friend, for once, will do the same
But then – he'll just 'step home to tell my dame'.
The surly squire at noon resolves to rule
And half the day – 'Zounds! Madam is a fool!'
Convinced at night – the vanquished victor says,
'Ah! Kate! you women have such coaxing ways!'
The jolly toper chides each tardy blade,
Till reeling Bacchus calls on love for aid:
Then with each toast, he sees fair bumpers swim,
And kisses Chloe on the sparkling brim!
Nay, I have heard that statesmen – great and wise –
Will sometimes counsel with a lady's eyes;
The servile suitors watch her various face,
She smiles preferment – or she frowns disgrace,
Curtsies a pension here – there nods a place.
Nor with less awe, in scenes of humbler life,
Is viewed the mistress, or is heard the wife.
The poorest peasant of the poorest soil,
The child of poverty, and heir to toil –

Early from radiant love's impartial light,
Steals one small spark, to cheer his world of night:
Dear spark! that oft through winter's chilling woes,
Is all the warmth his little cottage knows!
The wand'ring tar – who, not for years, has pressed
The widowed partner of his day of rest –
On the cold deck – far from her arms removed –
Still hums the ditty which his Susan loved:
And while around the cadence rude is blown,
The boatswain whistles in a softer tone.
The soldier, fairly proud of wounds and toil,
Pants for the triumph of his Nancy's smile;
But ere the battle should he list her cries,
The lover trembles – and the hero dies!
That heart, by war and honour steeled to fear,
Droops on a sigh, and sickens at a tear!
But ye more cautious – ye nice judging few,
Who give to beauty only beauty's due,
Though friends to love – ye view with deep regret
Our conquests marred – our triumphs incomplete,
Till polished wit more lasting charms disclose,
And judgment fix the darts which beauty throws!
– In female breasts did sense and merit rule,
The lover's mind would ask no other school;
Shamed into sense – the scholars of our eyes,
Our beaux from *gallantry* would soon be wise;
Would gladly light, their homage to improve,
The lamp of knowledge at the torch of love!

Dictionary of 'Malapropisms'

Act I, Scene ii

179 ' . . . *illiterate* him . . . from your memory,' – obliterate.
191 ' . . . don't attempt to *extirpate* yourself . . . ' – extricate.
192 'I have proof *controvertible* of it,' – incontrovertible.
213 'There's a little *intricate* hussy . . . ' – possibly ingrate.
218 ' . . . you are an absolute *misanthropy* – possibly misogynist.
239 ' . . . you surely speak *laconically* – ironically.
243 ' . . . a *progeny* of learning,' – prodigy.
284 ' . . . nothing is so *conciliating* to young people . . . ' – no direct
      transposition offers itself but 'unconciliating' would be more
      appropriate to the sense of the dialogue.
288 ' . . . not altogether *illegible*,' – ineligible.
297 ' . . . under my *intuition*,' – tuition.
312 'forfeit my *malevolence* for ever,' – benevolence.
313 ' . . . no excuse for your *locality*,' – loquacity.

Act II, Scene ii (Mrs Malaprop's letter).

32 'the first *superfluous* view . . . ' – superficial.
35 'give me joy *infallible* . . . ' – ineffable.

Act III, Scene iii

13 ' . . . the *ineffectual* qualities in a woman,' – intellectual.
25 'the very *pineapple* of politeness!' – pinnacle.
33 ' . . . I *exploded* the affair!' – exposed.
34 ' . . . my positive *conjunctions* . . . ' – injunctions.
36 ' . . . laid Sir Anthony's *preposition* before her . . . ' –
      proposition.
39 ' . . . it gives me the *hydrostatics* . . . ' – the hysterics.
40 'I thought she had *persisted*,' – desisted.

41   ' . . . I have *interceded* another letter . . . ' – intercepted.
70   ' . . . if I *reprehend* anything . . . ' – apprehend.
72   ' . . . a nice *derangement of epitaphs*!' – arrangement of epithets.
195   ' . . . headstrong as an *allegory* on the banks of the Nile,' –
      alligator.

Act IV, Scene ii

6   'No *caparisons*, Miss . . . ' – comparisons.
12   'His *physiognomy* so grammatical!' – phraseology.
47   ' . . . my *affluence* over my niece . . . ' – influence.
141   ' . . . the elegant *compilation* . . . ' – appellation.

Act V, Scene i

183   ' . . . suicide, *paracide* and simulation . . . ' – parricide.
185   ' . . . prevent the *antistrophe*!' – catastrophe.
187   ' . . . he *enveloped* the affair to me,' – developed (revealed).
202   ' . . . tell you the *perpendiculars*,' – particulars.
233   ' . . . should only *participate* things,' – precipitate.
240   ' . . . the Derby *putrifactions*!' – petrifications (fossils).
242   ' . . . the utmost *felicity*,' – velocity.
245   ' . . . gentleman will *exhort* us' – escort.
246   ' . . . our *envoy* – lead the way, and we'll *precede*,' – convoy,
      proceed.

Act V, Scene iii

187   ' . . . no *delusions* to the past . . . ' – allusions.
222   ' . . . thou barbarous *Vandyke* . . . ' – vandal.

Glossary

Allemandes – a German dance.

Anchorite – hermit.

Bays – laurel, as awarded to poets.

Bedlam – a corruption of 'Bethlehem', a famous asylum for the insane in London.

Blondes – silken lacework.

Bob – a style of wig.

Bumper – glass filled in preparation for a toast.

Carrots – colloquially, red hair or a red wig.

Cerberus – a three-headed dog which guarded the gateway to Hades (Greek myth).

Cit – derogatory term for a Londoner of the trading class.

Closet – a small, private room or, adjectivally, something that might take place there (see Sheridan's *Preface* – with 'an address to the *closet*' he refers to the fact that the Preface is meant for those who read the playtext in private, as opposed to attending a performance) .

Cotillon – a French dance.

Du Peigne – 'of the comb' (French); ie a dandy, or dandified.

Ensign – lowest rank of military officer: a 'half-pay ensign', one in receipt of his subsistence pay (approximately half full pay) only.

Farrier – blacksmith and/or horse doctor.

Firelock – musket.

Fire-office – office of a fire insurance company.

Fleet – Fleet prison in London, known for holding debtors.

Imposition – deception.

Jupiter – chief among the gods, who took various forms to seduce mortal women (Roman myth) .

Monkeyrony – corruption of 'macaroni', meaning a fop or dandy, and 'monkey'.

Mort – a large amount.

Paduasoy – a silk, corded fabric or garment made from it.

Phoebus – god of the Sun and of poetry (Greek myth).

Poltroon – abject coward.

Prometheus – the Titan who brought humankind the gift of fire (Greek myth).

Quinsy – inflamation of the tonsils and surrounding area.

Rout – party.

Scotch parson – one who, under the separate laws of Scotland, could marry couples under twenty one years of age .

Simony – the sin of selling church preferments or benefits.

Sharps – duelling sword.

Smithfield – a London meat market: 'Smithfield bargain', a marriage based on money .

Snaps – corruption of 'snaphaunce', a type of flintlock pistol.

Stock – cravat.

Tambour – embroidery frame.

Toilet – a wash, or wash stand.

Toper – drunkard.

Thread-papers – papers used to separate threads in embroidery, or colloquially, to curl hair.

Ton – mode, fashion.

Turnspit – kitchen servant whose duty was to turn the cooking spit.